*Englisch lernen mit*



ROSAMUNDE PILCHER

# *Endings and Beginnings*

**Berlitz Publishing**
München • New York • Singapur

Berlitz Englisch lernen mit Rosamunde Pilcher
Endings and Beginnings

Vokabelerklärungen und Übungen: Sigrid Köhler
Lektorat: Anneke Richter
Layout: Ute Weber
Cover-Gestaltung: Dominik Lommer
Projektleitung: Eva Betz



Berlitz Publishing
Mies-van-der-Rohe-Straße 1
D-80807 München



Satz: Franzis print&media GmbH, München
Druck: CS-Druck CornelsenStürtz, Berlin
Printed in Germany
ISBN 978-3-468-79240-3

1. 2. 3. 4. 5. 12 11 10 09 08

# Inhalt

# Liebe Leserin, lieber Leser,

mit den romantischen Kurzgeschichten von Rosamunde Pilcher halten Sie endlich ein Englischbuch in der Hand, das Sie garantiert nicht mehr weglegen wollen. Und vor lauter Gefühlschaos und Spannung merken Sie vielleicht gar nicht, dass Sie ganz nebenbei auch Ihre Englischkenntnisse gehörig auffrischen und erweitern.
Damit Ihr Lesevergnügen nicht durch das Nachschlagen unbekannter Wörter gemindert wird, sind die schwierigsten Vokabeln im Text blau markiert und in der Marginalspalte übersetzt. Interessante Wörter, die in einer Infobox erklärt werden, sind zusätzlich mit einem Sternchen gekennzeichnet. Alle übersetzten Wörter sind außerdem im Wörterverzeichnis im Anhang zusammengefasst.
Allein beim Schmökern in den Kurzgeschichten können Sie sehr viel dazulernen. Vielleicht möchten Sie aber auch Ihr Grammatikwissen und Ihre Vokabelkenntnisse zusätzlich erweitern oder aber Ihr Textverständnis prüfen. Zu diesem Zweck finden Sie auf jeder Doppelseite knifflige und unterhaltsame Übungen. Die Vokabeln aus dem Text werden dort noch einmal verwendet und bleiben dadurch viel besser im Gedächtnis haften – so können Sie später leichter darauf zurückgreifen. Selbstverständlich sind auch die Lösungen zu allen Übungen im Anhang abgedruckt.

Und nun wünschen wir Ihnen viel Spaß beim Lesen!
Ihre Berlitz-Redaktion

## Endings and Beginnings

Abschiede

Tom said, without much hope, "You could come with me this weekend."
Elaine gave a derisory laugh. "Darling, can you see me freezing in a castle in Northumberland*?"
"Not really," he admitted, with honesty.
"Besides, I haven't been invited."
"That wouldn't matter. Aunt Mabel would love a new face around the place. Particularly one as attractive as yours."
Elaine tried hard not to look pleased. She adored compliments and absorbed them as blotting paper absorbs ink. "Flattery will get you nowhere," she told him. "And I'm very cross. You were meant to be coming down to the Stainforths' with me this weekend. What am I going to tell them?"
"Tell them the truth. That I've got to go north for my Aunt Mabel's seventy-fifth birthday party."
"But why do you have to go?"
He explained again, patiently. "Because somebody's got to put in an appearance, and my parents are in Majorca, and my married sister's living in Hong Kong. I've told you that three times."
"I still don't see why you have to leave me in the lurch like this. I don't like it." She gave him one of her most persuasive smiles. "I'm not used to it."
"I wouldn't leave you in the lurch," he assured her, "for anyone in the world but Aunt Mabel. But she's a very special old girl. Her husband, Ned, died some years ago and she doesn't have any children of her own. She was always so marvellous to us when we were young, and

lachte spöttisch

außerdem

gab ihr Bestes • liebte … über alles • Löschpapier • Schmeicheleien • sauer • solltest • zu … kommen

sich sehen lassen

verstehe • mich … hängen lassen • schenkte ihm eines ihrer verführerischsten Lächeln

unheimlich nett

she must have had to go to a lot of effort to organise any sort of shindig. I think it's very plucky of her. I would be churlish if I didn't turn up. Besides," he finished in truth, "I want to be there." He said again, "You could come with me."
"I shouldn't know anybody."
"You would, after you'd been there for five minutes."
"Anyway, I hate being cold."
He stopped trying to persuade her. It was always fun taking Elaine to places and introducing her around to his awestruck acquaintances. She was so sensational to look at that Tom's own self-esteem took a welcome boost. On the other hand, if she was not having a good time, she would make no effort to hide the fact.
Staying with Aunt Mabel was always a bit dicey. One's well-being and comfort depended heavily on the state of the weather, and if the coming weekend turned chilly or damp then Elaine, hothouse London flower, might turn out to be the worst possible companion.
Tom put his hand over hers. "All right," he said. "You don't have to come. I'll ring you when I get back and tell you all about it. And you'll just have to say I'm sorry to the Stainforths."

sich große Mühe gegeben haben • so ein • Remmidemmi • mutig • ungehörig • mich ... blicken lasse

sie ... vorzustellen • von Bewunderung ergriffen • Bekannte • Selbstwertgefühl • wohltuend gestärkt wurde • riskant • stark • würde • die Londoner Gewächshauspflanze • rufe dich an

**info** Northumberland ist eine Grafschaft in Nordostengland an der Grenze zu Schottland.

**Übung 1** Lösen Sie das Kreuzworträtsel mithilfe der Erklärungen.

**Down** (senkrecht)
**1** a wide road on which you can travel fast
**2** to bother someone
**3** brave

**Across** (waagerecht)
**4** a difficult situation
**5** to have a strong desire for something
**6** admiring

The next day was Friday. Tom, who had already squared things with his boss, left the office at lunchtime and headed north up the motorway. As he drove he was able to allow his thoughts a free rein. Inevitably they chose to chew over the problem of Elaine.
He had known her now for three months and, despite the fact that she frequently exasperated him, she was nevertheless the most engaging person he had met in years. Her very unpredictability he found delightfully stimulating, and she never failed to make him laugh. Because of this, he had taken her home once or twice for long weekends, not anticipating that his mother would find Elaine just as attractive as he did.
"She's perfectly charming," she kept saying, but she was a model mother and managed, with obvious effort, not to say more.
Tom, however, knew very well what she was thinking. He was, after all, nearly thirty. It was time that he settled down, got himself married, provided his mother with the grandchildren that she craved. But did he want to marry Elaine? It was a dilemma that had been teasing him for some time. Perhaps getting away from her for a little while would be the best thing that could

abgesprochen • fuhr nach • Autobahn • konnte ... seinen Gedanken freien Lauf lassen • zwangsläufig • sich mit ... auseinanderzusetzen • obwohl • auf die Palme brachte • die hinreißendste • gerade • Unberechenbarkeit • brachte ihn immer wieder zum Lachen • nichts ahnend • vorbildliche Mutter • nach denen sie sich sehnte • ihn ... gequält

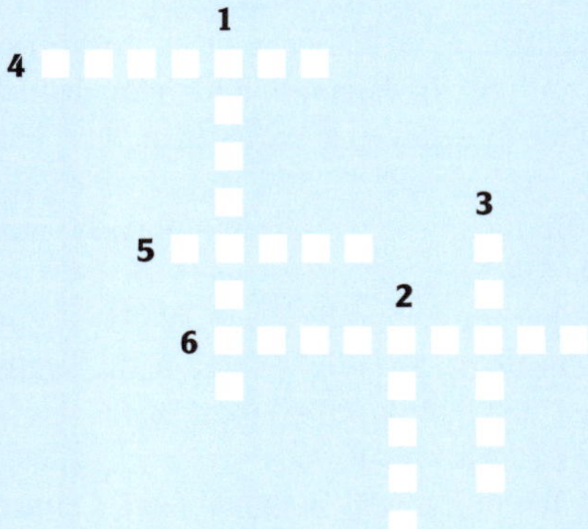

happen. He could view the problem at a distance, as though he were studying some complicated painting; get the details of their relationship into a true perspective. The best way to start doing this was to stop thinking about her, so he put visions of Elaine firmly out of his mind, and concentrated instead on the weekend which lay ahead.

Northumberland. Kinton. Aunt Mabel's party. Who would be there? Tom was the sole representative of his side of the family, but what about all the other cousins? All Ned's young relations, who had formed the larger part of that gang of children who had run wild at Kinton when they were all young? He ran a mental finger down an imaginary list. Roger was a soldier. Anne married and with a family. Young Ned was in Australia. Kitty … Putting on speed to overtake a thundering lorry, Tom found himself smiling. Kitty was Ned's great-niece. Kitty the rebel, the one who led the way. Kitty, who fell out of the tree-house. Kitty, who organised the skating party the night the lake was frozen. Kitty, who slept out on the battlements because one of the others had dared her, and because she thought she might see a ghost.

The rest of them over the years had, more or less, conformed. Taken typing courses and become secretaries. Been articled to chartered accountants or solicitors and finally qualified. Joined the Services. Kitty had conformed to nothing. In desperation her parents had sent her to a French family in Paris, as an *au pair*, but after Madame had found her being passionately embraced by Monsieur, she was given – unfairly, everybody agreed – the sack.

"Come home," her frantic mother had cabled her, but Kitty didn't come home. She hitched a lift to the South of France where she met up with a most unsuitable – everybody agreed again – man.

He was called Terence, a wild Irishman from County

aus der Ferne betrachten • sich … genau ansah • verbannte … aus seinen Gedanken

einzig • Gruppe • herumgetobt • ging … im Kopf durch • er beschleunigte • überholen • dahindonnernd • die Anführerin • Schlittschuhparty • im Freien auf den Zinnen • mit ihr gewettet • gingen in die Lehre bei … • Wirtschaftsprüfer • Rechtsanwälte • Waren in die Streitkräfte eingetreten. • in einer leidenschaftlichen Umarmung mit • wurde sie … entlassen • die außer sich war • ihr telegrafiert • trampte

Cork, and he ran a yacht charter service out of St Tropez. For a while Kitty had chartered yachts with him, and then brought him back to England to meet her parents. The opposition to him had been so deadly and so absolute that the inevitable happened and Kitty married him.

"But why?" Tom had asked his mother when he heard this incredible news.

"I've no idea," said his mother. "You know Kitty better than I do."

"She was the sort of person," Tom had told her, "that you could lead with a carrot, but who wouldn't re–spond to the spur."

Once, on the way back to London after a weekend in Sussex, he had gone to see Kitty and her husband; they lived on a houseboat and Kitty was pregnant. The boat, and Kitty, had both been in such a state of shambles that Tom, without having meant to, asked Kitty and her husband out for dinner. It had been a disastrous evening. Terence had got drunk; Kitty had talked, non-stop, as though she had been wound up; and Tom had said scarcely anything at all. He simply listened, paid the bill, and helped Kitty get Terence back on board.

betrieb • von ... aus

heftig • Unvermeidliche

mit Zuckerbrot locken • auf die Peitsche reagieren • schlimmer Zustand • zum Abendessen eingeladen hatte • katastrophal • hatte sich betrunken • aufgezogen • kaum

**Übung 2**

Was bedeuten die folgenden Wendungen aus dem Text? Kreuzen Sie die richtige Erklärung an.

**1.** The opposition to Terence had been strong.
☐ disapproval of ☐ approval of ☐ dislike of

**2.** Tom hadn't meant to ask Kitty and her husband out for dinner.
☐ intended to ☐ wanted to ☐ remembered to

**3.** Kitty had talked as though she had been wound up.
☐ very upset ☐ very sad ☐ very anxious

Then he had left her and driven back to London. Later he heard that the baby had been a boy.

Once, when he was in his teens, Mabel had told Tom that he should marry Kitty. He had bucked from the very idea, partly because she was like a sister to him, and partly because he was embarrassed, at nineteen, even to be talking about such things.

"Why do you say that?" he had asked Mabel.

"You're the only person she's ever taken any notice of. If you told her to do something, or not to do it, then she'd behave herself. Of course those parents of hers have never known how to deal with her."

"She's so bouncy, she'd wear me out," Tom had said. He was just going to Cambridge and bouncy sixteen-year-olds like Kitty had no place in his plans.

"She won't always be bouncy," Aunt Mabel had pointed out. "One day she'll be beautiful."

sich schon bei dem Gedanken gesträubt

zur Kenntnis genommen hat

sprunghaft • wäre mir zu anstrengend • waren ... nicht vorgesehen

The road unrolled like a great ribbon behind him. He was through Newcastle and now deep into Northumberland. He left the motorway and headed into the country, through hilly moorland and small stone villages, and down steep avenues of beech. By now it was

breitete sich ... aus • wie ein breites Band

Buchenalleen

**Übung 3** Sind die folgenden Aussagen wahr oder falsch? Tragen Sie ein T für true oder ein F für false in die Kästchen ein.

1. ☐ Tom felt like returning to London as he didn't want to go north without Elaine.
2. ☐ The time without Elaine would help Tom to get a different perspective on their relationship.
3. ☐ Tom's cousin Kitty had been a rebel in her youth but in the end she became a chartered accountant.
4. ☐ Tom had been surprised to hear that Kitty of all people had got married.

late afternoon. The sun was setting in a blaze of pink, casting rosy shadows on the undersides of large, wet-looking clouds.
He came at last to Kinton, rounded the squat, square-towered church and the main street of the village stretched before him. It was an unremarkable street: two rows of small houses, little shops, a pub. It could have been anywhere. Except that, at the far end of this street, a cobbled ramp climbed a grassy slope and passed beneath the arch of a magnificent gatehouse. Beyond the gatehouse was a high-walled courtyard as big as a rugger pitch and on the far side of this stood the castle. Four storeys high, square and turreted with pepper-pot towers; romantic, unexpected, incongruous.
This was the home of Tom's redoubtable Aunt Mabel. The older sister of Tom's father, horse-mad, leathery and down-to-earth, Mabel had never been expected to find a husband. But when she was approaching thirty, love – or something very like it – had struck. She had met Ned Kinnerton, and was married to him within the month.
The members of her family had been, by all accounts, torn between delight and horror.

Glut • warf ... Schatten • fuhr um ... herum • gedrungen • wenig bemerkenswert • Auffahrt mit Kopfsteinpflaster • Hang • Pförtnerhaus • von hohen Mauern umgeben • Rugbyfeld • mit Zwiebeltürmchen • fehl am Platz • Respekt einflößend • zäh • bodenständig • auf ... zuging • eingeschlagen • laut Berichten

**5.** ☐ Aunt Mabel had always been so kind to him that there was no way he wouldn't travel up to her birthday party.

**6.** ☐ Tom and Kitty were only a year apart in age.

**7.** ☐ Kitty had always listened to what Tom had said.

**8.** ☐ Tom was convinced that Elaine and Kitty would get along being so alike.

**9.** ☐ Tom had some sad memories of his childhood days in Northumberland.

"Isn't it marvellous that she's found a husband at last?"
"He's twice her age."
"She's going to have to go and live in an enormous, unheated castle in Northumberland."

wunderbar • doppelt so alt wie sie

But Mabel loved Kinton as much as Ned did. Their union had not been blessed with children but, as though to make up for this slip of nature, a selection of nephews and nieces descended upon Mabel and Ned for their school holidays. Mabel never minded what anybody did, provided no one was ever unkind to an animal. So, unchecked, they climbed battlements, slept out in a make-shift tent beneath the cedar tree, poured make-believe boiling oil from the slit window over the massive front door, swam in the reedy lake, contrived bows and arrows, fell out of trees.
After Ned died, everyone imagined that Mabel would move out of Kinton. But the only male relation who might have been capable of shouldering the massive responsibility of the castle had already taken off for Australia and was making a good life for himself there, and so Mabel remained. "Don't need to heat all the

Verbindung • als eine Art Wiedergutmachung für • Ausrutscher der Natur • fiel ... bei ... ein • vorausgesetzt • unbeaufsichtigt • Zinnen • behelfsmäßig • Zeder • imaginär • Gusserker • schilfig • bastelten • auf sich zu nehmen • sich nach ... abgesetzt

**Übung 4** Vervollständigen Sie die Sätze, indem Sie die Lücken mit je einem der folgenden Wörter ergänzen (blessed, make-believe, make-shift, unchecked).

1. Fortunately the children were not supervised by the adults, they could play ______________.
2. The children pretended that the oil was real but it was just ______________.
3. They slept in a tent that was not the real thing, it was only ______________.
4. Aunt Mabel had not been ______________ with children of her own.

rooms," she pointed out and shut off the attics by means of draping thick, woolly blankets across the tops of the circular stairs.

Apart from that, life carried on as before. Still castle-fuls of children – now in their teens and fast growing up. Still immense meals at the long mahogany dining-table. Still dogs everywhere, smouldering log fires, tattered snapshots stuck into the frames of mirrors.

Kinton. Tom had arrived. He eased the car gently up the cobbled ramp, passed beneath the shadowed arch of the gatehouse.

On the far side was an immense, ragged lawn. The road separated, and ran around this on both sides, to meet again in front of the massive door. The encircling walls were part of the most ancient remains of the castle, and the crevices between their stones sprouted with wild valerian and wallflowers.

Tom parked the car and got out. The evening air smelt sweet and fresh but was cold after London. He went up the steps and grappled with the huge wrought-iron latch of the front door, and it swung slowly inwards, creaking slightly like a door in a horror film. Inside, the high, unheated hallway struck with a damp chill. The floors were stone, an immense fireplace stood flanked by dusty armour and crowned with a ring of ancient swords. He crossed this hallway and went through another set of doors, and now it was as though he had left the Middle Ages behind him, and was stepping into the Italian Renaissance.

When he had first come to Kinton as a small boy, expecting only spiral staircases and secret passages and small, darkly-panelled rooms, he had been flummoxed by all this opulence. He had looked forward to living in a medieval castle and felt slightly cheated. But when questioned, Ned had explained to him that one of Ned's Victorian forebears had taken as his wife a lady of great wealth, and one of her conditions for mar-

Dachgeschoss • indem sie • Wendeltreppe • eine Burg voller

glimmend • Holzfeuer • abgegriffen • Schnappschüsse • fuhr ... ganz langsam ... hoch • mitgenommen • teilte sich

Überreste • Spalten • aus ... wucherten • Baldrian • Goldlack • kämpfte mit • schmiedeeisern • Riegel • schlug ihm ... entgegen • Kälte • aus Stein • Rüstungen

Wendeltreppen • dunkel getäfelt • war ... erschlagen von • Pracht • mittelalterlich • ein bisschen • Vorfahren

rying him was that she should be allowed a free hand with the interior of the castle.

eine Menge • Paradestück • Pracht • entwarfen • getäfelt • Gänge • Säulenfenster • Florenz • Ankleidezimmer • Wandgemälde • Gipströge • scharlachrot

She had subsequently spent five years and a great deal of money in transforming Kinton into a showpiece of pseudo-Renaissance splendour. Interior walls, as much as possible, were ripped away. Architects devised the enormous curving stairway, the wide, panelled passageways, the delicately arched and pillared windows. An Italian was imported from Florence to design and paint the highly decorated ceilings and to transform the walls of the heiress's boudoir, by means of a *trompe l'oeil** mural, into a Mediterranean terrace, complete with plaster troughs of scarlet geraniums.

einziehen

After all this structural work had been completed, it was still another six months before the young couple were able to take up residence. Wallpapers were chosen, curtains hung, new carpets laid in all the rooms. The Kinnerton portraits were hung on the dining-room walls, family mementoes were displayed in glass-fronted cabinets.

Familienandenken • Glasvitrinen

But since those days of mad extravagance, nothing very much had been done to Kinton. Nothing had been changed or renewed, although from time to time vari-

**info** Ein Trompe-l'œil täuscht im wörtlichen Sinne das Auge. Es ist eine Technik der Malerei, die Decken und Wände optisch vergrößert; in Mabels Ankleidezimmer schafft das ein Wandgemälde in Form einer Mittelmeerterrasse.

**Übung 5** In jeder Zeile steht ein Wort, das nicht zu den anderen passt. Streichen Sie es durch.

**1.** curtains – carpets – geraniums – wallpapers
**2.** renew – change – transform – display
**3.** subsequently – interior – structural – new

ous articles might be glued or nailed together, mended, repainted, or patched.
Fires smouldered in the grates of sitting-rooms, but the passages and bedrooms at Kinton were apt to be piercingly cold.
There was a smell: musty, familiar, dear. Tom ran up the curve of the staircase, taking the steps two at a time, his hand brushing lightly against the mahogany rail that had been polished to a sheen by generations of hands. At the top, he paused on the wide landing and listened. There was no definite sound, but he knew that Mabel would be somewhere around.

ausgebessert • geflickt • Kaminen • waren in der Regel • bitterkalt • moderig • vertraut • geliebt • auf Hochglanz poliert • Treppenabsatz

He found her in the library, wearing an apron and a hat, surrounded by the usual army of old and faithful dogs, as well as a litter of newspaper and flower stalks. She was constructing, in a priceless Chinese bowl, an elaborate arrangement of flowers.
"Oh, my dear."
She laid down her secateurs and enfolded him in her embrace, which was something of an experience as she was as tall as Tom and twice as wide. Then she stood back, holding him at arm's length.

Schürze • ein Haufen • Blumenstiele • stellte ... zusammen • von unschätzbarem Wert • Schale • kunstvoll • Gartenschere • Erlebnis • und hielt ihn von sich weg

**Übung 6**

Die folgenden Wörter aus dem Text haben je nachdem, in welchem Zusammenhang sie stehen, eine andere Bedeutung. Kreuzen Sie die richtigen Bedeutungen an.

| | | | |
|---|---|---|---|
| **1.** experience | ☐ Erfahrung | ☐ Experiment | ☐ Erlebnis |
| **2.** construct | ☐ bilden | ☐ bauen | ☐ zusammenstellen |
| **3.** landing | ☐ Landung | ☐ Ausladen | ☐ Treppenabsatz |
| **4.** elaborate | ☐ näher eingehen auf<br>☐ ausarbeiten | | ☐ kunstvoll |

Her face, he had always thought, was a man's face: strong-featured, large-nosed, square-chinned. This masculinity was emphasised by her uncompromising coiffure, her grey hair drawn tightly back and screwed into a straggling bun.

markant • mit eckigem Kinn • eigenwillig • Frisur • zu ... gedreht • unordentlich • Knoten

She said, "You're looking marvellous. Did you have a good journey? How splendid of you to come. Look at me, trying to make the place look presentable for tomorrow night. Can't describe to you what it has been like. Eustace – you remember my old gardener – he's been in, shoving furniture around, and his wife's polished everything in sight, including the dogs' bowls, and the kitchen's full of caterers. Hardly know my own house. How's your mother and father?"

hat ... herumgeschoben • in Sichtweite • Leute vom Partyservice

She picked up her secateurs and went on with her task while Tom, leaning up against a table, with his hands in his pockets, told her.

"Wretched creatures," she remarked, "going off to Majorca at a time like this. I really wanted them to be here. There!" She inserted the last flower and stood back to admire the finished result.

gemein

"Aunt Mabel, isn't all this a frightful lot of work for you?"

"No, not really. I just tell people to do things and they do them. It's called delegating. And we're not having a proper orchestra. Nobody knows how to waltz these days, so I've ordered a disco."

richtig • kann Walzer tanzen

"Where's it going to be?"

"In the old nursery. We emptied it of all the old toys and the doll's house and the books, and Kitty's decorating it to look like a jungle."

Kinderzimmer

After a bit, Tom said, "Kitty?"

"Yes. Kitty. Our. Kitty."

"She's here?"

"Of course she's here."

"But the last time I saw her – she was living on a houseboat."

"Oh, dear, you're very out of date. That marriage broke up. She got a divorce."
"What happened to Terence?"
"I think he went back to the South of France."
"And the little boy?"
"He's with Kitty."
"Is she staying here?"
"No, she lives at Caxford." Caxford was a village out on the moor, a few miles from Kinton. "She came to stay with me after the divorce, and then she bought this derelict cottage. Heaven knows what with, she doesn't appear to have two brass farthings to rub together. Anyway, she bought it and told us all that she was going to do it up and live there. With that, the council slapped a preservation order on it. I thought that would be the end of it, but she managed to get quite a good grant, and she's been there ever since, living in a caravan with Crispin."
"Crispin?"
"The boy. Nice little chap."
"But what is she going to do with herself?" Tom asked.
"Oh, goodness knows. You remember what Kitty was like, once she'd got the bit between her teeth, you

gar nicht auf dem Laufenden • ist zerbrochen • hat sich scheiden lassen

verfallen • womit • scheint keinen müden Pfennig zu besitzen • es renovieren • daraufhin • Gemeinde • hat es ... unter Denkmalschutz gestellt • Darlehen • Bursche • sich etwas in den Kopf gesetzt

**Übung 7**

Welche Präposition gehört zu welchem Wort? Ziehen Sie Linien.

| | |
|---|---|
| to rub | with |
| to do | on |
| to slap | up |
| to break | together |
| to stay | up |

could never get a word of sense out of her. Do you want tea?"

"No, I'm fine."

aufzuräumen • Abfälle

"I'll give you a drink later on." She began to clear up the litter of her flower arrangement, but as she did this, a knock came at the door, and an unknown head appeared.

"Mrs Kinnerton, it's the man with the glasses. Where do you want them to go?"

Räum ... auf • Scheit

"Oh, dear life, if it isn't one thing it's another! Tidy this up for me, would you, Tom, and put a log on the fire ..."

sie ging davon • gehorsam

And she took herself off.

Tom was left in the empty room. He dutifully threw a few dead flower stalks into the fire, added some logs and then went off to find Kitty.

Pendeltür • in ... gekleidet • Filz

The old nursery at Kinton was situated at some distance from the main rooms, and shut off from them by a swinging door studded in red baize. It was contained within the walls of one of the many towers and so was round, with two low-arched windows, and this in itself had made it fascinatingly attractive to small children.

**Übung 8** Entscheiden Sie sich für die richtige Antwort und kreuzen Sie sie an.

**1.** Mabel was told that the man with the glasses had arrived. Who was he?

- ☐ It was a man who brought glasses for the party.
- ☐ It was a man who was wearing glasses but was otherwise unknown.

**2.** What kind of place was the nursery at Kinton?

- ☐ A place where plants and trees were grown.
- ☐ A room where the children played.

Now it stood empty. The ceiling and the walls, however, had been draped with garden netting suspended from a central fixture in the roof, and this netting was woven with long strands of trailing ivy and sprays of evergreen.

As well, there was a tall pair of steps and on the top of these, with pliers gripped between her teeth and a ball of green string in her hands, was a tall and slender girl, her blonde hair scraped back into a ponytail and a look of agonised concentration on her face as she struggled with a recalcitrant branch of spruce.

As he came into the room, she took the pliers from her mouth and, without looking at him, said, "If somebody would just get this ivy out of my face …"

"Hello, Kitty," said Tom.

She turned, at some peril to her own safety, and looked down at him. The spruce branch fell to the floor and the ivy wound itself around her neck like some pagan wreath. After a few seconds she said, "Tom."

"You seem to be having a good time up there."

"I'm having a miserable time. I can't get anything to stay in place."

"It looks fine to me."

verhüllt • Gartennetz • das von … herunterhing • Halterung • Strängen • Efeuranken • Zweigen • hoch • Trittleiter • Kneifzange • schlank • zu einem Pferdeschwanz zurückgebunden • gequält • widerspenstig • Fichtenzweig • was nicht ungefährlich war • heidnisch • Kranz

**Übung 9**

Entwirren Sie den Buchstabensalat und setzen Sie die Wörter in die Lücken ein!

1. For practical reasons Kitty had tied back her hair into a ____________________. (tiolnypa)
2. The branch of spruce wasn't as flexible as Kitty wanted it to be, it was quite ____________________. (cetatnirracl)
3. Kitty was concentrating so hard, she actually looked as if she was in pain or ____________________. (donagesi)
4. The ____________________ was draped with garden netting. (igencil)

Cautiously, she disentangled herself from the ivy, tucked it away in the folds of the netting and then turned around and sat on the top step, facing him. She said, "I knew you would be coming. Aunt Mabel told me."

befreite sich • steckte es in • Falten • oberste Stufe

"I didn't know you were here."

"Nice surprise for you."

"You're thin. It suits you."

steht dir

"That's all my hard work. Have you heard about my house?"

"Mabel just told me. She told me about the divorce too. I'm sorry."

"I'm not. The whole thing was a ghastly mistake and one that I should never have made." She shrugged. "But you know me, Tom. If ever there was a stupid thing to do, then I did it."

furchtbar • zuckte mit den Achseln

"Where's your little boy?"

"Around the place somewhere."

She was wearing a dirty old pair of jeans and blue canvas sneakers. Her sweater was so old as to be ragged. There was a hole in one sleeve, and Kitty's elbow protruded from this. Looking up at her, he realised how much she had changed. Where once

Leinenturnschuhe • so ..., dass • ragte ... hervor

**Übung 10** Adjektiv oder Adverb? Übersetzen Sie das Wort in Klammern und setzen Sie es in der richtigen Form ein.

**1.** Kitty was very ______________ in disentangling herself from the ivy. (vorsichtig)

**2.** Kitty had worked very ______________. (schwer)

**3.** She knew it had been really ______________ of her to get married to Terence. (dumm)

**4.** ______________ she had married Terence. (dummerweise)

cheeks had curved above that stubborn chin, bones and planes and angles now showed. There were lines about her mouth, but the shape of that mouth was the same, with laughter hovering, and a dimple which appeared when she smiled.

She smiled now. Her eyes were intensely blue. He dragged his gaze away from her and searched for other things to talk about. He saw the complicated contrivance of garden net and greenery. "Did you do all this yourself?"

"Most of it. Eustace helped me get the netting up. It's going to be a disco. Isn't Mabel a marvel? Imagine having a disco at your seventy-fifth birthday party!"

"You've made a good job of it. It looks very night-clubby."

She said, rather wistfully, "How's London nowadays?"

"Same as ever."

"Have you still got the same job? With the insurance people?"

"So far."

"So far so good. And how's your love life? Isn't it time you were getting married? Not that I'm much of an example to follow."

"My love life is doing very nicely, thank you."

"I'm glad to hear it. Here!"

He caught the pliers that she threw to him, and the ball of string, and then went to hold the step-ladder steady while Kitty descended.

"Tell me about your house."

"Nothing to tell, really. We're living in a caravan."

"Will you show me the house?"

"Of course I will. You can come and see me tomorrow. I'll probably give you a job of work to do."

"Do you think if we went and made the right sort of noises somebody would give us a cup of tea?"

They turned off the light and made their way back across the landing and through the big door that led to

Ebenen • Kanten • Falten • immer zum Lachen bereit • Grübchen • zwang sich, von ... wegzuschauen • Konstruktion

Wunder

wehmütig

gut

Rolle Bindfaden • abstieg

besuchen • Arbeit

tüchtig • kulinarisch • gebraten • Eiweiß • schlug vor sich hin

Teigfetzen • sah ... unglaublich ähnlich

the kitchen. Here a couple of stalwart ladies were engaged in every sort of culinary preparation for the party the following day. A roasted turkey was just coming out of the oven; egg whites were beating in an electric mixer; soup steamed in an enormous pan. In the middle of all this, at the end of the long table, eating pastry scraps, sat Crispin. He looked amazingly like Kitty.

She introduced him.

"This is Tom, and he's a sort of cousin. I don't know whether you call him Tom or Uncle Tom or Cousin Tom or what."

"Just Tom," he said, pulling out a chair and sitting down. Kitty had joined the stalwart ladies at the other end of the kitchen.

"We live in a caravan," Crispin told him.

"I know."

"We're going to live in a house."

"I've been hearing about it. I'm going to come and see it."

"You're not allowed to walk on the floor because it's all sticky. Mummy's been varnishing it ..."

"It'll be dry by now."

klebrig • lackiert

**Übung 11** Welche fünf inhaltlichen Fehler haben sich in diesem Text versteckt? Streichen Sie sie an.

The kitchen was buzzing with activity. Several men and women were preparing food for Aunt Mabel's seventieth birthday party. Some were beating egg whites for a cake. Kitty's teenage son Crispin was busy eating leftovers. He told Tom that he and his mother lived in a caravan but that they were going to move in with Aunt Mabel after the party.

Kitty had wandered back again to inform them that a tray of tea had been taken into the library, so they trooped off and found Aunt Mabel sitting by the fire, sharing gingerbread with four tail-waving dogs.

Tom slept that night in a brass bedstead, in a bedroom that had only a single dim light hanging from the middle of the ceiling and a howling draught which whistled across the floorboards. Investigation disclosed the fact that this was coming from a hole in the roof of an adjoining tower room, where a row of coat hooks and some wire hangers indicated that this was the closet where he was expected to put his clothes. Tom, unpacking, did this, got into his pyjamas and then made the long journey to the nearest bathroom in order to clean his teeth. Finally he got into bed. The sheets were linen, much darned and icy to touch, the pillowcase so heavily embroidered he knew that he would awake in the morning with the pattern embossed upon his cheek.
It rained in the night. He awoke and lay listening to it; first a patter of drops and then a steady drumming on the roof and then, inevitably, the drip, drip, drip of the

Tablett mit • zogen ... ab • Pfefferkuchen mit Ingwergeschmack • schwanzwedelnd • Messingbett • trüb • heulend • Durchzug • pfiff • Dielen • ergaben, dass • angrenzend • Kleiderhaken • Drahtbügel • Schrank • aus Leinen • mehrfach • gestopft • Kissenbezug • üppig • bestickt • als Abdruck • Regentropfen • gleichmäßig

## Übung 12

Aufgepasst, wenn es ums Liegen (to lie – lay – lain) oder Legen (to lay – laid – laid) geht! Schreibweise und Zeitformen sind sich zum Verwechseln ähnlich.
Tom lag da und hörte dem Regen zu. = Tom lay listening to the rain. Aber: Bitte leg die Handtücher aufs Bett = Please lay the towels on the bed. Ergänzen Sie die richtige Verbform.

**1.** Tom was ______________________ on his bed.
**2.** He had ______________________ the pyjamas on top of his bed.
**3.** He liked to ______________________ there and listen to the rain.

leak in the tower room. He lay and thought about his dinner jacket hanging there, and wondered whether he should get up and rescue it, and then decided that he couldn't be bothered to leave his bed. He thought about Mabel, and tried to imagine how much longer she could continue to live in this vast and primitive place. He thought about Kitty and Crispin, cosy and warm in their caravan. He thought about Elaine and was glad, under such circumstances, that she had decided not to accompany him. He thought about Kitty again. That face … the mouth with the dimple when she smiled. Still thinking about Kitty, he went to sleep, lulled by the peaceful sound of the rain.

It had stopped raining by the morning. Tom awoke late and came downstairs to find a plate of bacon and eggs kept warm in the oven, and a flurry of domestic activity already in progress. Chairs were being shunted to and fro, crates of glasses manhandled up the stairs, tables set out, draped in immense damask cloths unused for years. Small vans burst into the forecourt through the arch of the gatehouse, to park at the front door and unload pot-plants, piles of plates, crates of wine, trays of freshly baked rolls.
One particularly disreputable van disgorged two long-haired young men and all the trappings of the disco. Tom left them, twined about with electrical wires, to set up their speakers and woofers and tweeters. Then, when he asked for a job to do, he was given the exhausting task of carrying big sackfuls of logs up the back stairs, as fuel for the many open fires.
Aunt Mabel was everywhere, large-footed, wrapped in a hessian garden apron, apparently tireless. On his fourth trip upstairs with a sack of logs on his back, Tom came upon her on the kitchen landing, peacefully mixing up dinners for her vast entourage of dogs as though it were the most important task of the day.

undichte Stelle • Smokingjacke
keine Lust hatte … zu
eingelullt von • Hektik • häuslich • hin- und hergeschoben • Kisten • verfrachtet • Damasttischdecken • brausten auf • Hof • Topfpflanzen • Brötchen • schäbig • entlud • das ganze Drum und Dran • Lautsprecher • Tief- und Hochtonlautsprecher • anstrengend • mit großen Füßen • aus Sackleinen • unermüdlich • traf auf • Absatz vor der Küche • Gefolge

He set down his sack and straightened his aching shoulders.
"This is worse than the salt mines. How many more of these do I have to bring up?"
"Oh, my darling, I'm sure you've brought enough. I didn't realise you were still doing it. I thought you'd stopped."
He laughed. "Nobody told me to stop."
"Well, stop now. Stop doing anything. There's nothing more to do, and if there is, somebody else can do it."
She looked at the massive watch on her wrist. "Go and buy yourself a drink in the pub. And have something to eat as well. The caterer doesn't provide luncheon, and I daren't go into the kitchen and cook for you, I'm sure I'd be turned out."
"I thought," said Tom, "I might drive over and see Kitty's new house at Caxford."
"What a good idea! You can take her out for lunch as well. I'm sure she never eats enough. I sometimes wonder if she ever eats anything. That's why she's got so thin. And as for that little Crispin, when he comes here he never has his hand out of the biscuit tin. Starved, most likely," she added tranquilly, and beamed down at her drooling dogs. "Who's ready for din-dins?"

schmerzend • ist ja schlimmer als Zwangsarbeit
riesig
sorgt ... fürs • Mittagessen • hinausgeworfen
Keksdose • gelassen • strahlte ... an • sabbernd • Fresschen

**Übung 13**

Ergänzen Sie die Wörter aus den folgenden Wortfamilien, die auch auf dieser Doppelseite zu finden sind:

| noun | verb | adjective |
|---|---|---|
| | to exhaust | exhausting |
| continuation | to continue | |
| drive | to drive | |
| progress | | progressive |
| | to imagine | imaginative |
| thought | to think | |

mit Blick auf ... in der Ferne • landeinwärts • vorherrschend • auseinandergezogen • hielt ... an • Torfgeruch • Blöken • Bauarbeiten • aufgewühlt

Caxford lay on the edge of the moor, with a distant view of the North Sea, and a small and beautiful church surrounded by trees which all leaned inland, away from the prevailing wind. Kitty's house lay at the far end of the main street, set away by itself, a little distant from the last straggling row of cottages. Tom drew up at the side of the road, got out of the car, smelt the peaty tang of the moor and heard the distant baa-ing of sheep. He saw the little house, the old walls and the new roof, the chaos of building that had churned up what had once been a front garden.

halb aus den Angeln hängend • sah sich ... um • begrenzende Weißdornhecke • Nebengebäude • Schweineställe • verbeult • Schubkarren

Tom carefully opened a sagging wooden gate and went up a stone path that led around the side of the house. At the back of it was a great deal more land. He looked about him with interest and saw the border hedge of hawthorn, a line of derelict outbuildings which had probably once been piggeries; in front of these was parked Kitty's caravan, which was serving as their temporary home while the cottage was being renovated, and a battered old car, along with a cement mixer and a selection of shovels and wheelbarrows.

Picking his way across the churned mud, Tom now had a view of the back of the house, and saw that on this

**Übung 14** Tragen Sie die gesuchten Begriffe in das Kreuzworträtsel ein.

**1.** a small house in the countryside
**2.** an other word for a teacher
**3.** a person legally owned by someone
**4.** thorny bush or tree with berries
**5.** a strong sharp smell
**6.** liquid painted onto wood
**7.** happy and optimistic

side a whole new extension had been constructed, the new roof tiles blending with the slope of the old. Planks led across pools of mud at the side of the house to the main door at the front, which stood open. It was a very beautiful panelled door of stripped pine and from beyond it came the cheerful sound of pop music. He made his way across the plank and banged on the door. "Kitty!"

The music stopped. She had switched off her transistor. A moment later she appeared at the door, looking much as she had looked yesterday except for a smear of brown varnish down one cheek.

"Tom! I didn't think you'd really come today."

"I said I was coming."

"I thought you'd be too busy helping Mabel."

"I've been working like a slave, but thank heaven she turned me out. She said I was to come and buy you lunch." He stepped through the door and looked about him with interest. "What are you doing?"

"I've just finished Crispin's bedroom floor."

"Where is Crispin?"

"He's gone to spend the day with the schoolmaster's family. They're terribly kind. My best friends, really.

Dachziegel • fügten sich in ... ein • Schräge • Bretter • Schlammpfützen • abgebeizte Kiefernholztür • dahinter hervor • schlug gegen die Tür • verschmierter Fleck • Lack

Lehrerfamilie

Tom thought it looked very

1. C ☐☐☐☐☐☐
2. ☐☐ H ☐☐☐☐☐☐☐☐
3. ☐☐ A ☐☐
4. ☐☐☐☐☐ O ☐☐
5. T ☐☐☐
6. ☐☐☐☐ I ☐☐
7. C ☐☐☐☐☐☐☐

The schoolmaster's wife is keeping him for tonight as well, and she says I can change for Mabel's party in her house, and have a bath. It's not very easy getting dressed for a dance if you're living in a rather cramped caravan."

"No, I can see that. When are you moving in here?"

"I think it ought to be ready in about two weeks."

"Have you got any furniture?"

"Enough. Enough for just the two of us to start with. It's just a cottage. Not very grand."

"It's got a frightfully grand front door, though."

Kitty looked delighted. "Isn't it beautiful? I got it from a scrap merchant. I got all the doors from scrap merchants or junk-yards. You know, people pull down lovely old houses because they're falling to pieces or somebody wants to build a factory in the garden, and sometimes somebody has the wit to save all the doors and the window frames and the shutters. This one was so handsome I immediately decided to make it my front door."

"Who stripped the paint off?"

"I did. I've done a lot of other things as well. I mean, the builders have done all the professional work, but they're terribly nice men and they don't seem to mind

ziemlich • beengt

prachtvoll • beeindruckend

Schrotthändler • Schrottplätze • reißen ... ab • baufällig sind • ist ... so schlau • Fensterläden • schön • hat ... abgebeizt

**Übung 15** Die folgenden Wörter sind Gegenteile von Wörtern aus dem Text. Um welche handelt es sich?

**1.** to build
**2.** ugly
**3.** spacious
**4.** to get undressed
**5.** to throw away
**6.** unpleasant

having me under their feet all the time. And if you have to pay people to strip paint off doors it costs the earth and, you see, I haven't got very much money. Anyway, come and look round. This is the kitchen, and we're going to have to eat in here as well, so it's got to be a kitchen-dining-room ..." Kitty explained.

Slowly they inspected the house, going from room to room, and Tom's natural interest grew to a sort of amazed admiration, for Kitty had somehow managed to see in a derelict cottage the possibilities of creating a house that was unique. Every room had its charming, unexpected feature. An odd little window, a recess for books, a soaring tongue-and-grooved ceiling, a sky-light.

The kitchen was flagged with red quarry tiles and an open stair rose to Crispin's attic bedroom, which had a long, low window where his bed would be, so that he could watch the sun rising in the mornings.

The sitting-room had not only a small and charming Victorian fireplace but a gallery as well, with access by means of a ladder which Kitty had had riveted to the wall.

"That's where Crispin can go to watch television. He can get away by himself and not have to be quiet when I have friends in."

A fire burned and crackled cheerfully in the grate.

"I lit the fire to see if it would draw properly."

"Was the fireplace here?"

"No. I rescued that from a dump, too, and set the blue and white tiles in around it. I think it looks just right, don't you?"

She showed him a pine dresser that she had bought and was going to fill with coloured china. She showed him a chair that she had made from a barrel, sawn in two. She showed him her own bedroom, which was on the ground floor and had French windows leading out on to what would one day be a terrace.

kostet ... ein Vermögen

reizvoll • Note • skurril • Nische • hoch • mit Spundung • Oberlicht • mit ... gefliest • Sandsteinfliesen • im Dachgeschoss • Galerie • die man ... erreichen konnte • an ... hatte anbringen lassen • Freunde zu Besuch habe • zieht • richtig

Müllhalde

Anrichte aus Kiefernholz • bunt • Porzellan • Fass • gesägt • Terrassentüren

Ziegelsteinhaufen • in Ordnung bringen • umgraben • scheußlich • Bettgestelle • Kultivator

He stood and looked out at the churned mud and the piles of bricks. "Who's going to put the garden straight for you?"

"I'll do it myself. I'll have to dig it, because there are all sorts of hideous treasures buried there. Like old bedsteads. I thought of putting a cultivator through it, but I think a cultivator would be broken in a matter of minutes."

He said, "Are you going to live here with Crispin?"

"Of course. What else do you think I would do?"

Weiterziehen.

"Sell it. Make an enormous profit. Move on."

"I couldn't sell it. I've put too much of myself into it."

"It's very isolated."

"I like it."

"And Crispin? What will happen to him? Where will he go to school when he's older?"

sah sie an • dir zu viel aufgeladen • begegnete ... seinem Blick • verblüffend

"Right here, in the village."

He turned from the window and faced her. "Kitty, are you sure you haven't taken on too much?"

For a moment she met his gaze; her eyes were enormous in her thin face, their blueness startling. Then she turned away from him.

**Übung 16** Welche Antwort ist richtig? Tragen Sie ein T für true oder ein F für false in die Kästchen ein.

**1.** Why is Tom worried about Kitty?

- ☐ He thinks Kitty is physically too weak to do the work.
- ☐ He feels she has taken on too much.

**2.** Why does Kitty have to dig the garden?

- ☐ She has to unearth all the things that are buried.
- ☐ The cultivator has broken down after the first try.

"Look, Tom, these are my fitted cupboards. See how huge they are. And I've only got one pair of jeans and a dress to put in them, I'm afraid. But you see, we used old shutters for the doors. They're really lovely, aren't they?"
She laid her hand on the satiny, honey-coloured wood, and it was like watching a person caress some living creature. "There's this pretty plaster moulding. At first I thought it was carved wood and I nearly rubbed it off ..." He saw her hands, the nails broken, the skin roughened and engrained with dirt.
"Kitty, are you sure this is what you really want?"
She did not at once reply to this. He waited and after a little she said, "In a moment, Tom, you're going to say, 'Kitty, you don't want to live here.' It's what people have been saying to me all my life. 'Kitty, you don't want to ride that horse.' 'Kitty, you don't want to buy that old bicycle.' 'Kitty, you don't want to wear that dreadful dress.' Whatever I really wanted to do, my parents always told me that I didn't. How could they know? It wasn't any good telling them that I didn't want to go to Paris and be an *au pair* girl, but if I hadn't gone, then I'd have been sent to some dismal place to

Einbauschränke

Fensterläden

seidig • liebkoste • lebendiges Wesen • Gipsornament • Holzschnitzerei • abgeschmirgelt • mit tief sitzendem Schmutz

es hatte keinen Zweck • trostlos

**3.** Why is Kitty so short of money?

- ☐ Two of the reasons are Crispin's school fees and paying off debts.
- ☐ After the divorce she was left with little money.

**4.** Why is Kitty estranged from her parents?

- ☐ She is very different from what they would have liked her to be and they never truly accepted her.
- ☐ They have distanced themselves after her divorce.

be taught how to cook or type or arrange flowers. I'm not that sort of person, Tom. That's why, when I got chucked out of that job in Paris – and it wasn't my fault, Monsieur didn't seem to be able to keep his hands off me and when Madame caught him at it, I was obviously to blame! – I didn't come home. I knew that if I didn't escape then, I never would. And as for Terence, my ex-husband … if only everybody had just left me alone, I know I'd never have married him. But it started right away, just as soon as they'd set eyes on him. 'Kitty, you don't want to have anything to do with a man like that.' 'Kitty, you don't want to marry him.' So in the end, I did. It's as simple, and as stupid, as that."

rausgeworfen wurde
ihn dabei erwischte • war … schuld
ihn zu Gesicht bekommen

Tom leaned his shoulders against the cold glass of the French windows, and put his hands in his pockets. He said, cautiously, "I wouldn't ever tell you what you want. I wouldn't know what you want. I just don't want to see you make another mistake, get into a situation that's way over your head."

vorsichtig
dich völlig überfordert

"I've been making mistakes all my life, but still, I must be allowed to go my own way. I've got Crispin and I don't need a lot of money. And I like it here in Caxford. I like being near Mabel. I like being near Kinton and remembering all the fun we had when we were children."

"I'm filled with admiration for you," Tom said. "I'm astonished at what you've achieved, Kitty. I just can't bear to think of you struggling on endlessly on your own …"

geschafft

"You mean the house? But that's been a sort of therapy. It's got me over Terence." She closed the doors of her cupboards and turned the latch, as though she were shutting Terence away. "You know, Tom, when I knew that you were coming north this weekend, I wished that you weren't. I didn't want to be reminded of that terrible evening when you took us out for dinner and

hat mir über … hinweggeholfen
an … erinnert werden

Terence got so drunk. I suppose it makes me feel embarrassed and ashamed. Nobody ever likes to feel ashamed. Or guilty." ist mir peinlich

"You have nothing to feel guilty about. I think you've come through a long dark tunnel, all on your own, and you're still in one piece, and you've got Crispin. As for Terence, well, you can simply write him down to experience." ihn … als … abschreiben

"Then you don't think this house is another mistake?"

"Someone who never made a mistake never made anything. And even if it is a mistake, it's a magnificent one. As I told you before, I'm filled with admiration."

"You mustn't say that. You mustn't be too kind."

He realised, with some surprise, that she was on the edge of tears. He could not remember ever having seen Kitty cry. kurz davor war zu weinen

"I'm … I'm not used to people being so kind …"

"Oh, Kitty …"

"It's just talking about it. Even Mabel thinks I'm insane. I haven't been able to talk to anybody. Not like this. Not to someone like you." verrückt

"You mustn't cry."

"I know, but I can't help it."

**Übung 17**

Vorsicht beim Erinnern! Im Englischen verwendet man to remember, wenn man sich selbst erinnert, und to remind, wenn man jemand anderen an etwas erinnert oder an etwas erinnert wird.

Ergänzen Sie die Sätze mit dem richtigen Wort.

**1.** Kitty didn't want Tom to ____________________ her of the evening when he had invited her and Terence for dinner.

**2.** Tom didn't ____________________ Kitty ever having been so upset.

**3.** They both ____________________ the happy days of their childhood.

suchte ... nach • hilflos • Taschentuch • sie nicht fand

ansprint

verantwortungslos

dass du dich von ... loslöst

es ... aushalten • ging durchs Zimmer • mager • Pullover • Tränen passen nicht zu dir • zugrunde geht • will nicht ... sein

She felt helplessly for a handkerchief which did not materialise, and he gave her his own and she blew her nose and wiped her eyes.

"It's just that so many things have gone wrong that sometimes – like this winter – when I'm tired and the car won't start, and the caravan's icy cold, and there's nowhere for Crispin to play ... I lose confidence in myself and begin to wonder if I'm really as irresponsible as everybody keeps telling me I am. 'Kitty, you don't want to bury yourself in Northumberland.' 'Kitty, you must think of Crispin.' 'Kitty, you're so selfish to cut yourself off from your family.' 'Kitty, what are you doing with your life?'"

Tom could bear it no longer. He crossed the floor, turned her towards him and pulled her into his arms. He could feel the skinny ribs beneath the wool of her sweater, and her hair was soft beneath his chin.

He said, "Don't cry any more. I don't associate you with tears and having you cry makes me feel that the world is falling to pieces."

"I don't mean to be so stupid."

"You're not stupid. I think you're fantastic. You're beautiful, you've survived and you've got your child.

## Übung 18

Welche Sätze oder Satzteile gehören zusammen? Tragen Sie den entsprechenden Buchstaben in die Kästchen ein.

1. ☐ As a teenager
2. ☐ He couldn't bare seeing her so upset.
3. ☐ Kitty needed various things for her house.
4. ☐ There where times
5. ☐ Aunt Mabel had always thought they would make a nice couple.
6. ☐ Kitty, Tom and the other nephews and nieces

That's what I think. And I need a drink. Let's go down to the pub and sit by the fire and talk about cheerful things, like summer coming and Mabel's party. And after we've had something to eat, I'll take you for a drive, and we'll go and walk on the moor; or we'll go down to the beach and throw pebbles into the sea, or we'll go into town and find an antique shop and I'll buy you something marvellous for your house. Whatever you'd like to do, Kitty. You only have to say the words. You only have to tell me ..."

Dusk was falling as he drove back to Kinton. The first of the lights came on as he turned the corner of the village street, and the castle loomed ahead of him, silhouetted against a turquoise sky.
It was odd to realise that tonight, perhaps for the last time ever, Kinton would be *en fête*. Lights would shine and music would play. Cars would roll through the arch of the gatehouse, their headlights flashing on the ancient walls. The old and shabby rooms, flower-filled and soft with candlelight, would ring with voices and laughter.
But never again. It was a miracle that the old ways had

Kiesel

es dämmerte • um die Ecke fuhr und in ... bog • erhob sich • als Silhouette • türkisfarben • zum allerletzten Mal • feiern • Scheinwerfer • voller Blumen • von Stimmen und Gelächter hallen

**a)** Kitty was too young and too bouncy for Tom at the time.
**b)** had made up for the fact that Mabel and Ned had no children of their own.
**c)** Tom wanted to take her to an antique shop and buy her something.
**d)** Kitty had been one of the wildest of the children.
**e)** He took her in his arms and comforted her.
**f)** when Kitty was close to giving up.

endured so long. Kinton was a ridiculous, out-dated anachronism, perhaps, but no more of an anachronism than Mabel herself. It was she who had achieved so much by sticking to what she believed in; by knowing what she wanted out of life; by being prepared to pay for it. She had turned the castle into a home, filled it with other people's children, seen only beauty in the cold lofty rooms. She had tended her garden, walked dogs, gathered friends around her fireside. She had, by some stubborn contrivance, managed to hold together the tattered fabric of threadbare carpets and recalcitrant boilers and crumbling walls. She had been, for so long, indomitable.

daran festgehalten hatte

hoch • sich um ... gekümmert • Hunde ausgeführt • durch sture Findigkeit • ausgefranst • Material • abgetreten • aufsässig • unbezwingbar

Driving slowly down the street, up the ramp and through the arch, Tom thought about that word, indomitable. And it occurred to him, then, that Kitty and Mabel had a lot in common. They were both unconventional to the point of eccentricity, their actions incomprehensible to ordinary beings. But they were survivors, too. In one way or another, whatever happened, instinct told him that they would both survive.

durchschnittlich

**Übung 19** Die folgenden Sätze enthalten je einen grammatischen Fehler. Finden und korrigieren Sie ihn.

**1.** The castle was always full of other peoples' children.
**2.** Mabel had helded it all together for a long time.
**3.** She had stuck to what she believed into.
**4.** Kitty and Mabel were very similar in much ways.
**5.** Deep in thought Tom drove back slow to Kinton.

He was in his bedroom, standing at his dressing-table and trying to tie his bow tie in the inadequate light, when there came a tap at his door.
"Tom."
He turned. It was Mabel. She looked magnificent in a long brown dress of old-fashioned cut, with family diamonds in her ears and the pearls Ned had given her on their wedding day around her neck.
Tom stopped struggling with his bow tie. He said, "You look wonderful," and meant it.
She closed the door and came towards him. "You know, Tom, I feel rather wonderful. Quite youthful and festive. Do you want me to help you with your tie? I always used to have to do Ned's for him, poor man. He was incapable of deciding which end was which."
Tom, who had already made his decision, stood obediently while she dealt with it for him. "There," she gave the finished effort a little pat. "That's perfect."
They stood looking at each other, smiling broadly.
He said, "Perhaps this is as good a time as any to give you your present." He went to take it from the top of the dressing-table, a large, flat parcel, painstakingly wrapped in crisp white paper and tied with a flourish of gold ribbon.
"Oh, Tom, you are a dear boy. You shouldn't have brought me anything. Just having you here is quite gift enough."
But she carried it, in obvious pleasure and anticipation, to the bed, where she sat herself down and proceeded to undo the wrappings. He went to sit beside her. The ribbon and the paper fell away; the old print, mounted and framed, was suddenly revealed.
"Tom! Oh, Tom, it's Kinton. Where did you find it?"
"By some extraordinary chance, in an antique shop in Salisbury. There were two or three in a sort of job-lot and this was one of them." He recalled the pleasure he had had in buying them, in finding such a perfect

Frisierkommode • Fliege • unzureichend • es an seiner Tür klopfte • Schnitt

kam zu ihm

festlich

und lächelten übers ganze Gesicht • sorgfältig • glatt • mit einem aufwendigen Goldband zusammengebunden • gespannt • machte sich daran • das Geschenk auszupacken • aufgezogen • kam ... zum Vorschein • Restposten • dachte daran, wie er sich gefreut hatte

present for Mabel. "I took it back to London and got it mounted and framed there."

She peered at it short-sightedly because, with her evening gown, she was not wearing her glasses. "It must be very old. At least two hundred years, I should think. How very kind of you. I shall be able to take it with me …"

"Take it with you?"

"Yes." She laid the picture carefully on the bed and turned to him. "I wasn't going to tell you tonight, but perhaps I will, after all. It's right that you should be the first to know. I'm going to leave Kinton. It's become, all at once, too much for me. It's too big and too old." She laughed. "Rather like me."

"Where will you go?"

"There's a small house in the main street of the village. I've had my eye on it for a little while. I shall do it up and put in some central heating, and the dogs and I will move there just as soon as possible, and live out the rest of our lives with the pork-butcher on one side and the newsagent on the other."

Tom, picturing this, smiled. He said, "I'm not surprised, you know. Sorry, but not surprised. Coming home

schaute … mit kurzsichtigen Augen angestrengt an

habe … ein Auge darauf geworfen • es herrichten • verbringen • Schweinemetzger • Zeitungshändler • stellte sich das vor

**Übung 20** Ergänzen Sie die fehlenden Konsonanten. Alle gesuchten Wörter kommen auf dieser Doppelseite vor.

**1.** Without her glasses Mabel could hardly see the print, she was __ e e __ i __ __ at it.

**2.** Mabel wouldn't have to walk far to do part of her shopping as she was going to live so close to the __ u __ __ __ e __.

**3.** The whole castle was in a bad state, from the tower to the __ a __ e __ e __ __.

this evening, driving down the street, I saw the castle and I knew then that there was no way it could carry on for very much longer."

"I'd have liked to die here. But then, I might have to be very ill and old first, and what a tiresome worry I should have been to all my good friends and relations."

"You've got years to go yet."

"I'm not sorry, you know. There comes a time to end everything; like leaving a party when you're really enjoying yourself. And we've had good times here, haven't we? It's so full of happy memories for me, and I would hate to sit around and grow old, and let them all turn stale."

"What will happen to Kinton?"

"I've no idea. Perhaps someone will want to buy it for a school, or a hospital, or a remand home, but I doubt it. Perhaps the National Trust* will take it over. Perhaps it will just crumble to bits. It's not far from that already. Dry rot in the basement. Death-watch beetle in the west tower." She laughed and struck him a loving blow on the knee. "Bats in the belfry*!"

Tom laughed with her. He said, "If you want to do up

es unmöglich noch ... so weitergehen konnte • lästig • Sorge • Verwandte

hast noch viele Jahre vor dir

schal werden

Jugendstrafanstalt • verfallen • Trockenfäule • Keller • Klopfkäfer

info

Der National Trust ist eine gemeinnützige Organisation, die unter anderem schöne Gebäude, Schlösser und Gärten von historischem Interesse in England, Wales und Nordirland betreut. In Schottland gibt es eine eigene Organisation, den National Trust for Scotland.

Von jemandem zu sagen, er oder sie hat bats in the belfry, heißt wörtlich, dass derjenige „Fledermäuse im Glockenturm" hat; es geht also um eine Person, die „nicht ganz klar im Oberstübchen" ist oder eben ein bisschen spinnt.

the house in the village, why don't you ask Kitty to help you?"

"Oh, yes," said Mabel. "I thought we'd come round to the subject of Kitty sooner or later."

"That little house of hers … I was wordless with admiration. The work she's put into it absolutely beggars belief."

"I know. She's a maddening, pig-headed child, but one has to take off one's hat to her."

"She's not as tough as she likes people to think."

"No. She's been through a bad time. After the divorce, I asked her and Crispin to live with me for a little, but she wouldn't. She said she had to sort out her own mess for herself." She fell silent. Tom, looking up, found himself on the receiving end of her thoughtful, calculating gaze.

Before he could speak, Mabel asked him, "What did you do today, you and Kitty?"

"Looked at the house. Had lunch in Caxford, drove into town and did some shopping. I bought her some blue and white Spode plates for her dresser. Then I took her home."

"You were always very close to Kitty. I think perhaps you were always the only person, who really understood her."

"You told me once that I should marry her."

"And you said that it would be incestuous because she was like a sister to you."

"And you said that one day she would be beautiful."

"And you told me that you'd be able to wait."

"I've waited," said Tom.

Mabel sat, vastly patient, waiting to see if he was going to enlarge upon this. When he didn't, she simply said, "Don't wait too long."

From far away, in the depths of the castle, came the faint sound of music. They listened. As though in deference to the occasion of the party, the long-haired

Thema • sprachlos • spottet … jeder Beschreibung • zum Verrücktwerden • dickköpfig • den Hut vor ihr ziehen • zäh • sich am eigenen Schopf aus dem Sumpf ziehen • schwieg • sah er, wie sie ihn … betrachtete • prüfend

(hochwertiges englisches Porzellan) • standest … nahe

inzestuös

mit Engelsgeduld • näher darauf einzugehen • leise • aus Respekt vor • Anlass

boys with the disco had chosen to start off this particular evening with a selection of Strauss waltzes.
Mabel was pleased. "How pretty! But I thought," she added, as though the complicated stereo system was an instrument on which the two young men were going to perform, "that they could only play rock and roll music."
He was about to explain when there came yet another knock at the door of his room.
"Mabel!"
"I'm in here, come along."
The door opened slowly, and Kitty's head appeared around the edge of it. Tom got to his feet.
"Mabel, I've been looking for you everywhere. You'll have to hurry. The first cars are beginning to arrive and you've got to be downstairs to greet your guests."
"Heavens!" Mabel heaved herself off the bed, tidied her bun, smoothed down the brown lace front of her skirt. "I had no idea it was so late." She looked keenly at Kitty. "And when did you get here?"
"About five minutes ago. Oh, Mabel, you look marvellous. But do hurry. You've got to be there."
"I'm on my way," said Mabel. She gathered up her pic-

Du liebe Zeit! • hievte sich vom • brachte ... in Ordnung • strich ... glatt • Spitzenvorderteil • eindringlich

**Übung 21**

Wie lautet das Adverb der folgenden Adjektive? Aufgepasst, nicht immer wird ein -ly angehängt!

| adjective | adverb |
|---|---|
| marvellous | |
| keen | |
| complicated | |
| slow | |
| late | |

ture and the paper and the golden ribbon. She kissed Tom on the cheek and made for the door, kissing Kitty *en passant* in an abstracted sort of way, and then was gone, her back erect, her diamonds flashing, her brown lace trailing on the threadbare carpet.

ging zur Tür

aufrecht • funkelten • zog hinter ihr her

Across the room, Tom and Kitty smiled at each other. Tom said, "Mabel is not the only one who looks marvellous." Kitty wore a dress so utterly romantic and feminine that she was, all at once, a totally different person. Slipper satin, white and pale blue, with a skirt that rustled when she moved and a neckline cut low to reveal her delicate shoulders, her vulnerable neck. Her pale, thick hair, clean and shining and very fair, hung in a soft curtain to frame her face and there were pearl studs in her ears and a tiny jewelled watch encircling one of her narrow wrists.

"Where on earth did you get that lovely creation? It's sensational."

"It's terribly old. I had it when I was eighteen and my mother was trying to turn me into a deb."

Tom smiled. "Come in and shut the door. I'm not ready yet, but I won't be a moment."

ausgesprochen

Atlasseide • raschelte • Ausschnitt • verletzlich • Hals • Perlenohrstecker • juwelenbesetzt • schmal • Handgelenke

aus mir … zu machen • Debütantin

## Übung 22

In diesem Buchstabendickicht sind acht englische Wörter versteckt. Sie sind senkrecht (von oben nach unten), waagerecht (von links nach rechts) und diagonal (von links oben nach rechts unten) angeordnet. Viel Spaß beim Suchen!

Die deutschen Entsprechungen der Wörter lauten

| | |
|---|---|
| rascheln | gebrechlich |
| Handgelenk | Druck |
| Ausschnitt | Schlüssel |
| winzig | krank |

She did as he said, coming to sit on the bed where Mabel had sat. She watched while he put on his shoes, picked up his jacket and put that on too, disposed of money and keys and handkerchief in various pockets. She said, "What did you give Mabel for a birthday present?"

entledigte sich

"A print of Kinton. She says she's going to take it with her."

"Where is she going to take it?"

"To a small house in the village. She's leaving the castle."

After a little, "I thought she might be," said Kitty.

"I don't know whether I was meant to tell you or not. You don't need to say anything."

"I'm just full of wonder that she's stuck it out – living here, I mean – so long. I ... I'm glad that she's going, though."

durchgehalten hat

"So am I. Like she said, it's best to leave a party while you're still enjoying yourself. And she doesn't want to become ill or infirm, and so an anxiety to all her friends."

gebrechlich • Sorge

"If she does become old and infirm," said Kitty, "then I shall look after her."

"Yes," said Tom. "Yes, I believe you will."

| | | | | | | | | | | | |
|---|---|---|---|---|---|---|---|---|---|---|---|
| i | w | n | b | t | i | b | t | x | z | q | o |
| e | i | r | u | s | t | l | e | q | w | z | v |
| r | v | n | i | s | i | k | s | p | o | t | t |
| g | d | n | u | s | y | e | r | v | b | e | s |
| v | i | e | j | m | t | m | w | e | d | l | e |
| p | s | c | r | k | i | m | p | v | w | z | i |
| n | a | k | g | i | n | f | i | r | m | t | l |
| o | p | l | s | l | y | f | w | y | i | a | i |
| u | p | i | f | v | e | z | j | u | i | n | p |
| p | e | n | h | k | e | y | j | i | t | e | t |
| k | a | e | i | w | e | n | i | l | l | p | r |
| y | r | f | h | p | n | c | y | l | w | m | l |

From below them, the music still played. But now, as well, there was the sound of cars approaching, of voices mingling.

Stimmengewirr

He said, "We should go down. We should be there to give Mabel some moral support."

"All right," said Kitty.

She stood up, smoothing down her skirts as Mabel had done, and Tom took her hand and together they went out of the room and down the long passage to the head of the stairs.

Now the music sounded more clearly. *Tales of the Vienna Woods.* Side by side, they started down the stairs. But as they descended, rounding the curve beneath the beautiful arched window, the hall below them revealed itself. He saw it, candlelit and firelit, the flickering flames reflected in the curved surfaces of dozens of champagne glasses lined up upon a table.

Geschichten aus dem Wienerwald.

Suddenly it was a moment so important that he wanted to savour it, to spin it out, to remember it for always. He stopped and held Kitty back. "Wait," he told her.

She turned to look at him. "Why, what is it, Tom?"

"There'll never be an instant quite like this again. You know that, don't you? We shouldn't hurry away."

ihn auskosten • in die Länge ziehen • Augenblick • es nicht so eilig haben

## Übung 23

In jeder Zeile steht ein Wort, das nicht zu den anderen passt. Streichen Sie es durch.

**1.** curve – arch – sound – hall

**2.** to descend – to go down – to smooth down – to start down

**3.** candle – champagne – fire – flame

**4.** splendour – joy – pleasure – satisfaction

**5.** blue – funny – enormous – unblinking

"What should we do?"
"Enjoy it."
He lowered himself down on to the wide lap of the stone stair and drew her down beside him. She sat, sinking down in a whisper of satin skirts, wrapping her arms about her knees. She was smiling at him, but he knew that she understood. A combination, perhaps, of everything that could fill him with pleasure and satisfaction. The time, the place and the girl.

setzte sich • Absatz • mit raschelnden Seidenröcken

Kitty – whom he had known for the best part of his life and yet had never known at all. She was part of it all; part of this evening, part of Kinton. He looked about him, at the painted ceiling, the soaring splendour of the arched window, the perfectly proportioned curve of the stone staircase upon which they sat together. He looked into her face and all at once was filled with joy.

fast sein ganzes Leben lang

He said, "When are you going to move out of your caravan and into your house?"
Kitty began to laugh.
"What's so funny?" Tom asked.
"You. I thought you were going to come out with something enormously flattering or romantic."
"I'm keeping the romance and the flattery for later on in the evening. But this is the moment for humdrum affairs."

alltäglich

"All right. I told you, in about two weeks."
"I was thinking … if you could wait for a month, I'm due for a few days off. I thought I might go to Spain, but I'd much rather come to Northumberland and perhaps give you a hand with your move. That is … if you'd like me to."

habe ein paar Tage Urlaub

dir … beim … helfen •

Kitty had stopped laughing. Her eyes were unblinking, enormous, very blue. She said, "Tom, you must never be sorry for me."

schauten ihn unverwandt an

"I couldn't be sorry for a person like you. I might admire, or be envious, or even be maddened. But pity would never come into it."

mich … totärgern

"You don't think we've known each other for too long?"

"I don't think we've known each other nearly long enough."

"I've got Crispin."

"I know you have."

"If you did come and help me – and I can't think of anything I'd like more – and at the end of it, you decided you'd had enough ... I mean I wouldn't want you to feel that I wasn't able to be on my own ... be independent. Couldn't do things for myself ..."

"You know something, Kitty? You're floundering."

"You don't understand."

"I understand perfectly." He took one of her hands and sat looking at it. He thought of Mabel and Kinton. Kinton a ruin, and Mabel and the dogs living in a small centrally-heated house and probably warm for the first time in their lives. He remembered Kitty as a child sleeping out on the battlements for a dare, stubborn and resolute and brave, and he thought of her son lying in his bed in their new house and watching, through the window, the sun rise.

Kitty's hand was scratched and rough and broken-

at the end of it: am Ende
're floundering: stammelst
for a dare: als Mutprobe
scratched: zerkratzt
broken-: die Fingernägel abgebrochen

**Übung 24** Welche der Antworten ist die richtige? Tragen Sie ein T für true oder ein F für false in die Kästchen ein.

**1.** Why is Kitty floundering?

- ☐ She is not sure of her feelings for Tom.
- ☐ She knows Tom is still in another relationship.
- ☐ She is afraid he feels pity for her and might change his mind.

nailed, but he thought it beautiful. He raised it to his lips, planted a kiss in her palm and folded her fingers over it.

fand sie

"What's that for?" she asked him.

"Endings," he told her, smiling. "And beginnings."

**2.** Why is Mabel going to leave Kinton?
- [ ] She has decided to retire in France.
- [ ] The castle is too big for her and in need of a lot of repair.
- [ ] Someone has made her a good offer for it.

**3.** Why is Tom ready to change his life for Kitty?
- [ ] She reminds him of his happy childhood.
- [ ] He realises that he feels happy, full of joy and satisfied in Kitty's presence.
- [ ] Aunt Mabel has convinced him that she is the right partner for him.

## Flowers in the Rain

Through thick, wetting mist and a cold east wind, the slow, stopping country bus finally ground its way up the last incline towards the village.
We had left Relkirk an hour before and, as the winding road climbed up into the hills, the weather had worsened, turning from on overcast but dry afternoon, to this sodden cheerless day.
"Aye*, it's driech*," the conductor commented, taking the fare from a fat country woman with a pair of carrier bags filled with her morning's shopping. And the very word, 'driech', took me back into the past and made me feel that I was almost coming home.
The window was misty with condensation. I rubbed a patch clear and looked out hopefully; saw stone walls, the vague shapes of silver birch and larch. Small turnings led to invisible farmsteads, lost in the murk, but by now I recognised the road and knew that in a moment we should cross the bridge and draw, at last, into the main street of the village.
I was sitting by the window.
"Excuse me," I said to the man next to me. "I have to get out at the next stop."
"Oh, aye." He heaved himself out of his seat and stood in the aisle to let me pass. "It's no' a very good day."
"No. It's horrible."
I made my way to the front of the bus. We crossed the bridge and the next moment were there, halted by the pavement in front of Mrs McLaren's shop.

Nebel • in jedem Dorf haltend • Überlandbus • ächzte ... mühsam ... hoch • Steigung • hatte sich verschlechtert • bedeckt • nass • ja • trostlos • Fahrgeld • Tragetüten • beschlagen • wischte mir ... frei • Stelle • Weißbirken • Lärchen • Abzweigungen • Gehöfte • dicker Nebel

kein

hielten ... an • am Bordstein

Gemischtwarenladen

*Effie McLaren*
*Lachlan General Stores*
*Post Office*

ausstiegen • knirschend • leiser geworden • Plätschern • Blöken • Rauschen • Kiefern • Hang • wunderbar

read the sign over her door, as it had read ever since I could remember. The door of the bus opened. I thanked the conductor and stepped down, followed by one or two other passengers who were alighting.
"Aye, aye," we all agreed. "It is a terrible day."
They went their separate ways but I stayed where I was, standing on the pavement by the bus stop. I waited until the bus pulled out; until the sound of its grinding engine had died away, up and around the next bend in the road. The silence filled up with other sounds. The bubbling, watery chuckle of the river. The bleat of unseen sheep. The sough of wind through the pines on the hillside above me. All blessedly familiar. Unchanged.

I and my three brothers had first come to Lachlan one Eastertime, with our parents, when I was about ten. After that the holiday became an annual event. Our home was in Edinburgh, where my father was a schoolmaster, but both my parents loved fishing, and each

**info**

Aye (ja) und driech (trostlos) sind schottische Dialektwörter, die in ganz Schottland verstanden werden. In Nord-, Mittel-, Südschottland und auf den Orkney- und Shetland-Inseln werden ansonsten unterschiedliche und sehr ausgeprägte Dialekte verwendet, bei denen man als Nicht-Einheimischer oft nachfragen muss. Gesprochen wird mit einem starken Akzent. Das ch in driech werden Sie nur in Schottland hören, es entspricht dem deutschen Laut. So wird Ihnen die Aussprache leichter fallen als manchem Engländer.

year rented the same little cottage from Mrs Farquhar who lived in what was always known as the 'Big Hoose'.

They were wonderful times. While my mother and father sat by the river, or for hours in a boat in the middle of the loch, we children were left to our own devices running wild over the heathery hillsides, swimming in icy pools, guddling for trout, or hiking, professionally haversacked, to some distant beauty spot. As well, we were absorbed into the local village life. My father sometimes played the harmonium in the Presbyterian church on Sunday mornings; my mother was asked to demonstrate Italian quilting to the Women's Rural Institute, and my brothers and I were included in school outings and concerts.

But the best – and this added real glamour to our yearly excursions – was the endless hospitality of Mrs Farquhar herself. A widow, and quite elderly, she genuinely loved people and there was always a selection of friends, their children, nephews and nieces, perhaps a godchild or two, staying in the house.

But only one grandson, the only son of Mrs Farquhar's only son.

Haus

See • uns selbst überlassen • heidekrautbewachsen • fingen ... mit den Händen • Forellen • mit Rucksäcken ausgerüstet • schöner Fleck • Quilten • Landfrauenverein • Schulausflüge • Glanz • wirklich • Patenkind

**Übung 25**

Bilden Sie die Pluralformen der folgenden Wörter, die auf dieser Doppelseite vorkommen. Achten Sie auf unregelmäßige Formen!

| | |
|---|---|
| trout | bus |
| godchild | person |
| church | country |
| picnic | life |
| tea-party | heather |

von Anfang an • Vergnügen • Schnitzeljagd

We were, from the first, automatically included in any ploy that might have been planned. Perhaps tennis, or a tea-party, or a paper-chase, or a picnic. I remembered how the front door of the Big House stood, always, open; the dining-room table laid for the next generous meal; the fire in her sitting-room always lighted, blazing and welcoming. I think of daffodils and I think of the Big House at Lachlan at Eastertime. Drifts of them in the wild garden, bowlfuls of them indoors, filling the rooms with their heavy scent.

lodernd • einladend • Osterglocken • Teppiche • schwer • Duft

When I told my mother, over the telephone, that I was coming to Relkirk to work for a month, she had said at once, "I wonder if you'll be able to get up to Lachlan."

"I'm sure they'll give me a day off. They'll have to, some time, or I'll collapse. I can catch a bus and make a visit. Go and see Mrs Farquhar."

"Yes ..." My mother didn't sound too sure about this.

"Why shouldn't I go and see her? Do you think she wouldn't remember us?"

"Darling, of course she would and she'd adore to see you. It's just that I don't think she's been awfully well ... I heard something about a stroke, or a heart attack. But perhaps she's better now. Anyway, you could always ring up first."

besonders • Schlaganfall

anrufen

But I hadn't rung up first. Presented with a day to myself, I had simply got myself to the bus stop in Relkirk and boarded the country bus. And now I was here, standing like a lunatic in the driving rain and already drenched. I crossed the pavement and went into the post office; the bell above the door went ting, and I was met by the familiar smell of paraffin mixed with oranges and cloves and the sugary smell of sweets.

als ob ich nicht ganz bei Sinnen war • peitschend • machte „Ting“ • mir schlug ... entgegen • Paraffin • Nelken

The shop was empty. It was always empty. It always had been empty, unless there were actually some customers there, buying stamps or chocolate, or cans of peaches, or button thread. Mrs McLaren preferred to

Knopflochgarn

live in her back room, beyond the bead curtain, where she drank cups of tea and talked to her cat. I could hear her now. "Well, now, Tiddles, and who will that be?" A few shuffling steps and she appeared through the beads, with her flowered pinafore and her brown beret, worn well down over her eyebrows. We had never seen her without that beret. My brother Roger insisted that underneath it, she had no hair, was as bald as Kojak*.

Perlenvorhang

schlurfend • geblümt • Kittelschürze • Baskenmütze

"Well, and what a terrible day it's turned into. And what can I be doing for you?"

I said, "Hello, Mrs McLaren."

She eyed me across the counter, frowning. I pulled off my woollen hat and shook out my hair and at once recognition dawned in her face. Her mouth opened in delight, her hands went up in the classic gesture of astonishment. "And if it isn't Lavinia Hunter! What a surprise. My, you've grown! However long is it since you were last here?"

Ladentheke • Wollmütze • sah man, dass sie mich erkannte

du meine Güte

"It must be five years."

"We've missed you all."

"We've missed coming, too. But my father died and my mother went to live in Gloucestershire, near her sister. And my brothers seem to be living all over the world."

**info**

Kojak war ein New Yorker Polizist in der gleichnamigen amerikanischen Fernsehserie. Die Figur wurde von Telly Savalas gespielt, dessen Glatze zu seinem Markenzeichen wurde.

**Übung 26**

Auf welche Wörter oder Ausdrücke im Text beziehen sich die folgenden Erklärungen?

**1.** oh my goodness
**2.** a covering for the head that is knitted out of wool
**3.** great pleasure or enjoyment
**4.** to change and become something different

"I'm sorry to hear about your father. He was a dear man. And how about yourself? What are you doing?"

"I'm a nurse."

"But that's splendid. In a hospital?"

"No. I was in a hospital. But now I do private nursing. I'm with a family in Relkirk, just for a month, helping to look after two older children and a new baby. I'd have been up to see you all before, but it's not very easy to get time off."

arbeite ... als Privatpflegerin

"No, no, you'll be busy."

"I thought I might go and see Mrs Farquhar."

"Oh, dear." Mrs McLaren's cheerful expression changed to one of sadness and gloom. "Poor Mrs Farquhar. She had a wee stroke and she's been going downhill, by all accounts, ever since. The house is changed now, not the way it used to be with all of you running around. Just the old lady upstairs in her bed, and two nurses, night and day. Mary and Sandy Reekie are still there, she doing the cooking and he taking care of the garden, but Mary says it's a chilling business cooking for just the nurses, for poor Mrs Farquhar takes no more than a wee cup of baby food."

Bedrückung • klein

keine schöne Angelegenheit

**Übung 27** Hier ist etwas durcheinandergeraten. Wer ist wer? Ordnen Sie die Namen der jeweils richtigen Beschreibung zu.

| | |
|---|---|
| Mrs Farquhar | the owner of the village shop |
| Rory | one of Lavinia's brothers |
| Mary Reekie | Rory's grandmother |
| Effie McLaren | Mrs Farquhar's cook |
| Roger | Mrs Farquhar's grandson |

"Oh, I am sorry. You don't think there's any point my going up to see her, then?"
"And why not? She might just be having a good day, and then, who knows the good it would do her to see a cheerful young face?"
"Doesn't anybody come to stay any more?" It was sad to think of the big house so bleak.
"Well, it wouldn't work, would it? Mary Reekie told me the one person Mrs Farquhar wanted to see was Rory, and she told the minister, too, and he wrote to Rory, but Rory's in America and I don't know if there was ever any reply to the letter."
Rory. Mrs Farquhar's grandson. What had prompted Mrs McLaren to suddenly come out with his name? I looked at her across the counter and tried to detect some glimmer of unexplained Highland intuition. But her faded eyes remained innocent and met my own with an untroubled gaze. I told myself that she could not guess at the pounding that started up in the region of my heart at the very mention of his name. Rory Farquhar. I had always thought of him as Rory, and will write of him that way, but in fact his name was spelt with Gaelic* inconsistence, R-u-a-r-a-i-d-h.

sich ... vorzustellen • trostlos
Pfarrer
dazu veranlasst • mit ... herauszurücken
unbekümmert • nicht erahnen konnte • Hämmern • bei der bloßen Erwähnung • gälisch • Ungereimtheit

info

Gaelic (= Gälisch) gehört zu den keltischen Sprachen und wird vor allem auf den Inneren und Äußeren Hebriden gesprochen. Auf einer Reise durch Schottland werden Sie viele Orts- und Straßenschilder sehen, die neben dem englischen auch den gälischen Namen tragen.

unvergessen

wahrnehmungsfähig • Geschirr • fesselnd • Neuen

I fell in love with Rory, one remembered sunny spring, when I was sixteen and he was twenty-two. I had never been in love before and it had the effect of making me, not dreamy, but intensely perceptive; so that objects, previously unnoticed, became beautiful; leaves and trees, flowers, chairs, dishes, firelight – everything was touched with the magic of a spell-binding novelty, as though I had never known any of these ordinary day-to-day things before.

Muße • ungezwungen • Auswerfen der Angel • Stückchen • Fliege • die Angel zu beschweren

There were many picnics that spring, and swimming in the loch and tennis parties, but the best was the idleness, the casual getting to know each other. Lying on the lawn in front of the Big House, watching somebody practising his casting, with a scrap of sheep wool instead of a fly to weight the line. Or walking down to the farm in the evenings to fetch the milk, or helping the framer's wife to bottle-feed the abandoned lamb who lived by her kitchen fireside.

räumten die Möbel aus • Reels • Kilt • drehte mich

At the end of those holidays Mrs Farquhar arranged a little party. We cleared the old billiard room of furniture and put on the record player, and danced reels*. And Rory wore his kilt* and an old khaki shirt that had belonged to his father, and showed me the steps and spun me till I was

**info**

Das Nationalbewusstsein der Schotten ist stark ausgeprägt. So lernen Kinder schon in der Schule schottische Volkstänze, wie den zu dritt oder viert getanzten Reel. Bei Hochzeiten und anderen Festen ist immer ein Reel dabei.

Die von Männern zu festlichen Anlässen, wie Hochzeiten und Bällen, getragenen Kilts sind, schlicht gesagt, Wickelröcke aus Wolle mit den verschiedenen Mustern (tartans) der jeweiligen Clans. Ab und zu wird Ihnen auf dem Land auch mal ein einzelner Schotte im Kilt auf der Straße begegnen, der ihn einfach aus Lust und Laune anhat.

breathless. It was at the end of that evening that he kissed me, but it didn't do much good because he was going back to London the next morning, and I could never be sure if it was a kiss of affection or a kiss of goodbye.

After he went I lived in a fantasy world of getting letters and phone calls from him, and having him realise that he could not live without me. But all that happened was that he started working in London, with his father's firm, and after that he did not come back to Lachlan for Easter. If he did take a few days off in the spring, Mrs Farquhar told me that he was going skiing, and I imagined rich and elegant girls in dashing ski-clothes, and felt sick with jealousy.

Once I stole a photograph of Rory out of an old album I found in a bookcase in Mrs Farquhar's library. It had come loose and fell out of the shabby pages, so it wasn't really stealing. I picked it up and put it in my pocket and later between the pages of my diary. I always kept it, although I never saw Rory again, and since my father died and we stopped coming to Lachlan, I had heard no news of him.

And now, Mrs McLaren said his name, and I remembered that young Rory, with his worn kilt and his brown face and his dark hair.

I said, "What's he doing in America?"

"Oh, some business or other, in New York. His father died too, you know."

"I expect Rory's a married man now, with a string of children."

"No, no, Rory never married."

We talked a little longer, and then I bought some chocolate from her, said goodbye and went out of the shop, and set off in the direction of the Big House. I tore the paper off the chocolate and bit off a chunk. Eaten thus, in the open air, it tasted just the way it used to.

'I'll just go and see,' I told myself. 'I'll just go and ring

affection: Zuneigung
dashing: todschick
felt sick with jealousy: war krank vor Eifersucht
come loose: sich gelöst
worn: abgetragen
string of: Haufen
chunk: großes Stück

mich hinauswirft • Kopftuch • Steppweste • in diesem ... Schlammgrün • musste • „Petri Heil“ • „Prost“ • einen hob • mit Gewalt dazu zu bringen • einträglich • Wohltätigkeitsveranstaltungen

at the door, and if the nurse sends me packing, it won't matter.'

A woman was coming towards me down the street, carrying a shopping basket and dressed in the country woman's uniform of headscarf, tweed skirt and sleeveless quilted waistcoat in that horrible sludgy green colour.

"I can't come all this way and not just try.'

She stopped. "Lavinia."

I stopped, too. It was certainly a day for being recognised. My heart sank. "Hello, Mrs Felham."

I *would* meet her. Stella Felham, the one woman in the village my mother could never bring herself to like. She and her husband, who had been a lawyer, had built themselves a house in Lachlan after his retirement and had settled permanently. He was a manic fisherman and always said "Tight lines" instead of "Cheers" when he took a drink, and she was enormously efficient and spent most of her time trying to dragoon the village ladies into attending philosophical lectures, or involving them in money-making events for charity. The village ladies were polite and charming but, despite Stella Felham's enthusiasm, the events were never very

**Übung 28** Was bedeuten die folgenden Ausdrücke? Kreuzen Sie die richtige Erklärung an.

**1.** Lavinia thought the nurse might send her packing.
- ☐ The nurse might tell her to pack her things.
- ☐ The nurse might tell her to go.
- ☐ The nurse might be rude to her.

**2.** Stella Felham ... I would meet her.
- ☐ Of all people I had to meet her.
- ☐ I expected to meet her.
- ☐ I thought I would meet her.

lucrative. She could never think why, and they were all far too kind to tell her.
"What a surprise! I couldn't believe it was you. What on earth are you doing here?"
I told her, as I had told Mrs McLaren.
"But my dear, you must come and see us. Lionel would love to have a glimpse of you." *Tight lines.* "Anyway, he's bored stiff today. He was meant to be fishing but it was called off."
"It … it's very kind of you, but actually I'm on my way to see Mrs Farquhar.
"Mrs Farquhar!" Her voice rose an octave. "But hasn't anybody told you? She's dying."
I could have hit her.
"Had this appalling stroke a couple of months ago. My dear, nurses, day and night. It's no good going to see her, she just lies like a log. We do what we can, of course, but I'm afraid social visiting is just a waste of time. So sad, when you remember how wonderful she was, and how much she's always done for the village. And as for that Rory – there he is, sitting in New York, and he's never been to see her. You'd think, when he'll obviously inherit the place …"

langweilt sich … zu Tode • wurde abgesagt

hat keinen Zweck • liegt da wie ein Stück Holz • Höflichkeitsbesuche

**Übung 29**

Vervollständigen Sie die Sätze mit den folgenden Wörtern (waste of time, rose an octave, bored stiff, glimpse, called off).

1. Stella Felham told Lavinia to come and visit as her husband had nothing to do and was ______________.
2. He would like to have a ______________ of Lavinia.
3. Lionel's fishing trip didn't take place as planned. It was ______________.
4. Mrs Felham was shocked to hear that Lavinia was going to visit Mrs Farquhar. Her voice ______________.

I couldn't bear to listen to anyone talking about Rory, and certainly not Stella Felham.
I said, "I am sorry. I really must be on my way. I haven't much time before the last bus back to Relkirk."
"You're going to the Big House, then?" She made it sound as though I were deliberately defying her.
"Yes, I am."
"Oh, all right. But if you have a moment to spare before you do catch the bus, be sure to pop in. Lionel will give you a snifter."
"So kind ..."
I backed away from her and then turned and left her standing there, gazing after me as though I were mad. Which I probably was.

absichtlich • mich ihr ... widersetzen
Gläschen
trat einen Schritt von ihr zurück

I wouldn't think about Rory, sitting in New York. If he hadn't come home, if he hadn't answered the minister's letter, there was probably some very good reason. I walked, in long, warming strides, on up the hill, along the narrow lane which led to the gates of the Big House. I came to them and they loomed before me, standing open. I did not walk up the drive, but took the short-cut through the wild garden, through the sodden drifts of daffodils. They were still in bud, closed against the rain, their trumpets unopened. I went beneath the trees and opened the tall gate in the deer fence. Beyond lay the rough grass, the azaleas and the hybrid rhododendrons, and then the lawn, sloping up to the gravel terrace in front of the house.
Through the mist the house took shape. The old, ugly, red stone house with the conservatory tacked on to one side and the pepper-pot turret over the front door. The outer door stood open and I went up the slope of the grass and crossed the gravel and went into the porch and rang the bell. Then, with the jangling of the bell still sounding from the back regions, I opened the inner glass door and let myself in.

Schritten, die mich aufwärmten
trieben ... Knospen • Wildgatter
Rhododendronkreuzungen • kiesbestreute Terrasse • Wintergarten • angebaut
Veranda • Klingeln • Tiefen des Hauses

It was very quiet. Very tidy. No flowers stood upon the table in the hall; no dogs barked; no children's voices broke the quiet. There was the smell of pine and polish and, as well, a faint aura of disinfectant, nursing, hospitals, so familiar to me that I noticed it at once. I went into the centre of the hall and pulled off my hat. I looked up the empty staircase. I said, not wanting to call too loudly, "Is anyone around?"

Möbelpolitur • Desinfektionsmittel

Out of the silence came footsteps, along the upper passage. Not the quick, rubber-heeled footsteps of a professional nurse but heavy, masculine footsteps. Sandy Reekie, I decided, upstairs to fill the log baskets for the invalid's fire. I waited.

gummibesohlt

The footsteps started downstairs. Reached the half-landing and stopped. He was silhouetted against the light of the stair window. Not Sandy Reekie, whom I remembered as wiry and stooped. But a tall man, dressed in a kilt and a thick sweater.

Treppenabsatz

drahtig • gebeugt •

"Who is it?" he asked, and then he saw me, my face tilted up to his. Our eyes met. There was a long silence. Then, for the third time that day, a person said my name. "Lavinia."

ich schaute schräg zu ihm hoch

And I simply said, "Rory."

## Übung 30

In allen gesuchten Wörtern steckt der Buchstabe a. Finden Sie die Wörter mithilfe der folgenden Erklärungen.

**1.** a room with glass walls and a glass roof that is built onto the side of a house: _ _ _ _ _ _ _ a _ _ _ _

**2.** an area between flights of stairs: _ a _ _ _ a _ _ _ _ _

**3.** a corridor: _ a _ _ a _ _

**4.** a knitted piece of clothing: _ _ _ a _ _ _

**5.** a cleaner that contains a chemical that kills germs: _ _ _ _ _ _ _ _ _ a _ _

He came on down the stairs, his hand trailing on the banister. He crossed the hall and took my hand.

Geländer

"I don't believe it," he said, and then he kissed my cheek.

"I don't believe it, either. Everybody tells me you're in New York."

"I flew over a couple of nights ago. I've been here a day."

"How is your grandmother?"

"She's dying." But he didn't say it the way Stella Felham had said it. He made it sound rather peaceful and nice, as though he were telling me that Mrs Farquhar was nearly asleep.

bei ihm hörte es sich ... an

I said, "I came to see her."

"Where from? Where have you come from?"

"Relkirk. I'm working there, nursing for a month. I got a day off. I thought I'd come to Lachlan. My mother told me Mrs Farquhar had been ill, but I thought perhaps she would be getting better."

als Pflegerin

"There are two nurses with her, around the clock. But the day nurse wanted to go and do some shopping in Relkirk, so I lent her the car and said I'd watch out for my grandmother." He paused, hesitating, and

kümmere mich um • hielt inne

**Übung 31** Sind die folgenden Aussagen wahr oder falsch? Tragen Sie ein T für true oder ein F für false in die Kästchen ein.

1. ☐ Lavinia is disappointed to get such a frosty reception from Rory.
2. ☐ Rory and Lavinia catch up on what has been happening in their lives.
3. ☐ Mrs Felham was the one who informed Rory that his grandmother was ill.
4. ☐ Rory was in New York when the letter with the bad news arrived.

then said, "There's a fire in the sitting-room. Let's go there. It'll be more cheerful. Besides, you're wet through."

völlig durchnässt

It was more cheerful. He put logs on the fire and the flames crackled up. I pulled off my wet anorak and warmed my swollen, scarlet hands at the blaze. He said, "Tell me about you all," so I told him, and by the time I had finished with all the family news I was truly warm again, and the clock on the mantelpiece struck four, so he left me by the fire and went off to put the kettle on for a cup of tea. I sat by the fire, very cosy and happy, and waited for him. When he returned, with a tray and cups and a teapot and the heel of a gingerbread he had found in a tin, I said, "And what about you? I've told you all about our family. Now you've got to tell me about you."

knisterten

Kaminsims

Endstück

"Not much to tell, really. Worked with my father for a bit and then, when he died, I went out and joined the American office. I was in San Francisco when my grandmother became so ill. That was why I've been so long in getting back."

deswegen hat es so lange gedauert, bis ich

"You had a letter from the minister."

I was pouring tea. He sat in an armchair and watched

5. ☐ Lavinia's parents used to rent a cottage from Rory's grandmother.

6. ☐ Apart from her present job as a private nurse Lavinia works in a hospital.

7. ☐ The sound of Rory's name evokes fond memories for Lavinia and makes her heart pound.

| | |
|---|---|
| die Gerüchteküche von Lachlan • Sie hat mehr Ärger gemacht, als sie wert ist. • bei ... aneckend | me, grinning. "Lachlan grapevine never gets anything wrong. Who told you that?" "Mrs McLaren in the shop. I also met Mrs Felham." "That woman! She's been more trouble than she's worth. Endlessly telephoning and rubbing the nurses up the wrong way, organising everybody, telling the Reekies what they ought to be doing." |

"She told me that Mrs Farquhar was lying like a log and there was no point in coming to see her."

"That's because she hasn't been allowed near the house, and she's furiously jealous if anybody else is."

meint es gut • erzähl weiter von

"I'm sure she means well. At least that's what my mother always used to say about her. Go on about America."

"Well, anyway, I had a letter from the minister, but I didn't get it until I returned to New York. I caught the first possible flight home."

"And if she ... when she dies ... what will happen to the house?"

"It'll come to me, and I'm very lucky. But what on earth am I going to do with it?"

erfolgreich • Bauer werden

"You could stop being a high-powered businessman and retire to the country and take up farming."

**Übung 32** Beim Leihen müssen Sie im Englischen achtgeben! So hat Rory einer der Krankenschwestern sein Auto geliehen: he lent her the car. Aber: the nurse borrowed the car from Rory.
Füllen Sie die Lücken mit dem richtigen Verb.

1. The nurse asked Rory: "Could you please ________________ me your car?"
2. Rory said: "No problem, you can ________________ it anytime."
3. Rory had no problem ________________ his car. (Bitte verwenden Sie hier die Verlaufsform!)

"Perhaps I'd end up like Lionel Felham, saying 'Tight lines' every time I took a drink."

I considered this. "No. I don't think you would."

He grinned again. "And farming is just about the most high-powered business that's going these days. I'd have to go back to college, start at the bottom, learn a whole new trade."

es ... gibt • heutzutage

"Lots of people do that. You could go to Cirencester. Take what they call the gin-and-tonic course. That's what people call the course for mature students, re–tired army officers, those sorts of people."

reif

"How do you know so much about it?"

"My mother lives no more than five miles from Cirencester."

He laughed, and all at once looked just as young as I had remembered him. "And then I should be near you all again. That's just about the biggest carrot you could dangle in front of this old donkey. I shall have to think seriously about it." And then he became grave again. "I would rather hold on to this place than anything else in the world. What good times we used to have. What good times we could have again. Remember walking down for the milk? And how you fed the lamb from a bottle?"

baumeln lassen • ernst

"I was remembering that."

"And the evenings when we danced reels ..."

We talked on, sharing memories, until the clock struck five. I could not believe the hour had passed so swiftly. I laid down my empty teacup and got to my feet. "Rory, I must go, or I'll miss my bus."

"I'd drive you back, only the nurse has borrowed the car, and anyway, I can't leave my grandmother." He hesitated. "Do you want to come up and see her?"

aber

I looked at him. I said, "I don't want to be like Stella Felham. I just wanted to see her again. I wanted to talk to her. I suppose, now, I just want to say goodbye."

He took my hand. "Then come," he said.

We went out of the room and up the stairs, hand in hand. Along the passage. At the end of the passage a door stood open, and now the hospital smell was stronger. We went through the doorway and into the big, pretty, faded bedroom, where Mrs Farquhar had slept since coming to Lachlan as a bride. Even with the familiar evidences of professional nursing, it was still a warm and welcoming room, essentially feminine with silver brushes on the dressing-table, photographs everywhere, frilled curtains drawn back from the long windows.

verblichen • Zeichen • Rüschenvorhänge

We went to the bedside. I saw her face, serene and beautiful still, the eyes closed, the wrinkled hand lying peacefully on the fold of the linen sheet. I took her hand in mine and it was warm, and I felt still that strong persistent throb of life. She wore a pale pink Shetland bed-jacket, lined with silk chiffon. A satin ribbon lay across her throat, provocative as if she had set it there herself.

heiter • beharrlich • Puls des Lebens • mit ... gefüttert • kess

Rory said, "Grandmother." I thought she was sleeping, but she opened her eyes and looked up at him, and then she turned her head and looked at me. For a moment those blue eyes stayed puzzled and empty, and then, slowly, came alive. Recognition sparked. Her fingers closed upon mine, a smile touched her wrinkled mouth, and quietly, but quite distinctly, she said my name.

verwirrt • Sie erkannte mich. (wörtlich: Erkennen zündete.)

"Lavinia."

We stayed only for a moment. We spoke, exchanging a word or two, and then her eyes closed once more. I bent quickly and kissed her. Her fingers loosened and I slipped my hand away and straightened up.

richtete mich auf

I said goodbye, but I didn't say it aloud. Then Rory put his arm around me and turned me, and we went out of the room and left her by herself.

I was in tears. I couldn't find a handkerchief but Rory had one, and he mopped me up, and finally I managed to stop crying. We went downstairs and back into the sitting-room, and I picked up my anorak and put it on. I pulled on my woollen hat. I said, "Thank you for letting me see her."

mopped me up: wischte mir die Tränen vom Gesicht

"You mustn't be sad."

I said, "I have to go. I have to catch that bus. Let me know what you decide to do."

"I will. When I've decided."

We went out of the room and across the hall and out through the open door. It was colder and wetter than ever, but the air smelt of heather and peat and across the sky, somewhere beyond the rain-clouds, an invisible oyster-catcher flew, crying his lonely song.

oyster-catcher: Austernfänger

"You'll be all right?" said Rory.

"Of course."

"You know the way?"

I smiled. "Of course." I put out my hand. "Goodbye, Rory."

He took my hand, and pulled me close, and kissed me. "I'm not going to say goodbye," he told me. "I'm going to say what the Americans always say. Take care. It doesn't sound so final. Just take care."

I nodded. He let go of my hand and I turned and walked away from him, down across the grass and into the misty tunnel beneath the trees, where the azaleas grew and the daffodils tossed their heads in the wind, waiting for the first of the sunshine, the first of the warmth.

let go: ließ … los

tossed: warfen

## The Blackberry Day

Brombeertag

The night train moved out of Euston*, heading north. Claudia, already changed into her nightgown and robe, pulled up the blind and sat on the edge of the narrow bunk, watching the city slip away, lights and dim streets and high-rise flats wheeling off into the past. It was a cloudy evening, the clouds stained bronze by a million street lamps but, as she watched, the clouds parted for a moment and a moon sailed into view, a full moon, round and shining as a polished silver plate.

Morgenmantel • zog … hoch • Rollo • Bett • Hochhäuser • gefärbt • bronzefarben

She turned off the lights, got into the bunk, with its cotton sheets all crisp and tight as a hospital bed, and lay and watched the moon and was lulled by the smooth, gathering speed of the train. Inevitably she recalled other, long-ago journeys and, for the first time, thought of tomorrow and felt a mild stirring of excitement. It was as though what she was doing had become a positive action, not simply a compromise. Not simply the next best thing.

zunehmend

This did something to bolster her bruised pride and enabled her to bundle, for the moment, anxious uncertainties out of her mind. They were still there and would remain so, lurking around the edge of her subconscious, but for the time being she allowed herself the luxury of knowing that she had taken the right course.

Auftrieb zu geben • verletzt • aus ihren Gedanken zu vertreiben • lauern • den richtigen Weg eingeschlagen

She was immensely tired. The moon shone into her eyes. She turned on her side, away from its disturbing brilliance, buried her face in the pillow and, surprisingly, slept.

schwül • verbraucht • über der sich ... wölbte • klar • Hauch • überbrückte • verstaute • Brosche • Aufschlag • weich • mit Reißverschluss

At Inverness she alighted from the train into a climate so different that the night train could have carried her not only north, but abroad. The day was Saturday, the month September, and she had left London on an evening warm as June, the air muggy and stale, the sky overcast. But now she walked out into a world that glittered in the early light and was arched by a high and cloudless sky of pale and pristine blue. It was much colder. There was the nip of frost in the air and leaves on trees were already turning autumn gold.
Here she had an hour or two to wait for the small stopping train that would carry her, through the morning, even further north. She filled this in by going to the nearest hotel and eating breakfast, and then walked back to the station. The news-stand had opened, so she bought a magazine and made her way to the platform where the smaller train waited, already gradually filling with passengers. She found a seat, stowed her luggage, and was almost at once joined by a pleasant-faced woman who settled herself across the table in the seat opposite. She wore a tweed coat with a Cairngorm* brooch in the lapel and a furry green felt hat. As well as her zipped overnight bag, she was burdened by a

**info**

Von Euston, einem der 14 Londoner Hauptbahnhöfe, fährt der Nachtreisezug nach Schottland.
Die Cairngorm Mountains sind eine Berggruppe im Nordosten von Schottland.

**Übung 33** Welches Wort passt nicht zu den anderen? Streichen Sie es durch.

**1.** stale – warm – pale – muggy
**2.** platform – passenger – luggage – newsstand
**3.** tweed coat – leaves – brooch – felt hat
**4.** to wear – to walk – to leave – to make

number of plastic shopping bags, one of which contained what looked like a hefty picnic. — deftig

Their eyes met across the table. Claudia smiled politely. The woman said, “Oh, my, what a cold morning. I had to wait for the bus. My feet turned to stone.” — sind eingefroren

“Yes, but it’s lovely.”

“Oh, aye, good and fine. Anything’s better than the rain, I always say.” A whistle blew, doors slammed. “There we are, we’re off. Sharp on time, too. Are you going far?” — knallten zu • es geht los • auf die Minute

Claudia, who had picked up her magazine, resigned herself to conversation and laid it down again.

“Lossdale.”

“That’s where I’m bound, too. I’ve been down for a night or two, staying with my sister. For the shopping, you know. They’ve a lovely Marks and Spencers*. Bought a shirt for my husband. Are you staying in Lossdale?” — Dahin bin ich … unterwegs.

She was not curious, simply interested. Claudia told her, “Yes, just for a week.” And then, because it was obvious that she would be asked, she volunteered the information. “At Inverloss, with my cousin, Jennifer Drysdale.” — gab sie … preis

**info**

Marks and Spencer, auch M&S genannt, ist eine erfolgreiche britische Kaufhauskette, die vor allem wegen ihrer Lebensmittelabteilung und Kleidung bekannt und beliebt ist.

**Übung 34**

Ergänzen Sie die fehlenden Formen der folgenden unregelmäßigen Verben aus dem Text.

| Present Tense | Past Tense | Past Participle |
|---|---|---|
| to bring | brought | |
| to know | | known |
| to lay | | laid |
| to blow | blew | |

"Jennifer! Oh, I know her well, we're on the Rural together. Stitching new kneelers for the Kirk. Funny she never mentioned the fact that you were coming."

"It was very much a last-minute arrangement."

"Is this your first visit?"

"No. I used to come up every summer when I was young. When her parents were alive, and before Jennifer inherited the farm."

"Do you live in the south?"

"Yes, in London."

"I thought so. By your clothes." The train was rattling over the bridge, the firth spread below them, stretching from the far western hills to the sea. She saw small boats going about their business, delectable houses facing out over the water with gardens sloping down to the shore. "I came up last night on the sleeper."

"That's a long journey, but better than driving a car. My man will scarcely go on the main roads these days, the traffic goes so fast. Like taking your life in your hands. But then he was always slow. It's his nature. Goes with his job."

Claudia smiled. "What is his job?"

"He's a shepherd. And his mind on not much else but his sheep. I just hope he remembers to come and pick me up at the station. I left a note over the cooker to remind him, but that's no certainty that he'll remember." She was not complaining. In fact, she looked quite smug about her husband's shortcomings, as though they made him special. "And is Jennifer coming to meet you?"

"She said she would."

"She's a busy girl, with the farm and the animals and the children. They're lovely bairns."

"I've only seen photographs. I haven't been to Inverloss for twenty years. Jennifer wasn't even married then."

"Well, she's got a lovely man in Ronnie. Mind, he comes from south of the border, but for all that he's a good farmer. Just as well, with that great place to run."

Landfrauenverein • Kniekissen • Kirche

ratterte • Förde

reizend

Nachtzug

Begleiterscheinung von

Herd

selbstzufrieden • Fehler

Kinder • zwar • Grenze (zwischen England und Schottland) • trotzdem • ist auch nötig

The conversation lapsed. Claudia gazed from the window. They were into the hills now, snaking away into a country desolate save for isolated farmsteads and flocks of sheep, and rivers flowing through wide green straths. The sun rose in the sky and long shadows grew shorter. Claudia's companion opened her picnic bag, poured tea into a plastic mug, munched genteelly on a ham sandwich.

The small stations came and went, the train idling for moments while passengers alighted or climbed aboard. They passed the time of day, and dogs barked, and porters trundled trolleys of parcels. Nobody hurried. It was as though there was all the time in the world.

The journey progressed and Claudia began to count the stops, as once she used to. Three more to go. Two more. One more. Nearly there. The train ran alongside the sea. She saw ebb-tide beaches and distant breakers. The shepherd's wife packed up her picnic, dusted shortbread crumbs from her pouter-pigeon bosom, rummaged in her capacious handbag for her ticket.

The train slowed, and the sign *Lossdale* sailed past the window. The two women stood, gathered up their belongings, stepped down on to the platform. The

lief aus • schlängelten sich • außer • Schafherden • Täler

kaute vornehm an • verweilte • Gepäckträger • schoben • Gepäckwägen • als ob sie alle Zeit der Welt hätten • Strände bei Ebbe • Wellenbrecher • wischte sich ... von • Butterkekskrümel • Kropftaubenbusen • kramte in • geräumig • Sachen

**Übung 35**

Die folgenden Wörter sind das Gegenteil von Wörtern auf dieser Seite. Finden Sie sie!

**1.** in a vulgar way
**2.** to get off
**3.** to get on
**4.** to unpack
**5.** close
**6.** to set
**7.** tiny

shepherd was there, with his dog. He had not forgotten, but greeted his wife with little fuss. "You're here," he told her unnecessarily, took her bag from her and strode away. She followed him, turning back to wave at Claudia. "See you around, maybe."

ohne viel Aufhebens

No sign of Jennifer. The train drew away and Claudia was left alone on the platform. She stood by her suitcase in her London suit, and decided that there is nothing more letting down than to have no person to meet one at the end of a journey. She determined not to become impatient. There was no hurry, no pressing appointment. Jennifer had just been held up …

nichts enttäuschender ist als • dringend

"Claudia!"

A man's voice. Startled, she turned, full into the sun, needing to shade her eyes. She saw him coming at her out of the dazzle, unrecognised for an instant and then, astonishingly, familiar.

erschrocken • aus dem grellen Licht

Magnus Ballater. The last person she had ever expected to see. Not forgotten, but out of mind for longer than Claudia cared to think about. Magnus, in dark corduroys and a hugely patterned sweater; taller and more heftily built than she remembered, with a head of unfashionably long, dark, thick hair, and that old

aus dem Sinn • wahrhaben wollte • groß gemustert • kräftiger • unmodern

**Übung 36** Hier ist die Reihenfolge durcheinandergeraten. Ordnen Sie die Sätze, indem Sie die Kästchen nummerieren. Der erste Satz gibt Ihnen Starthilfe.

- 1 Claudia shared the second part of her journey with a lady who kept her entertained.
- ☐ She approved of Jennifer's husband Ronnie even though he wasn't Scottish.
- ☐ Claudia was slightly disappointed.
- ☐ Magnus told Claudia that Jennifer hadn't been able to collect her because of a problem with the boiler.

irrepressible grin on his suntanned, weather-seamed face.
"Claudia."
She knew that she was gaping, and had to laugh at her own amazement. "Magnus. For heaven's sake. What are you doing here?"
"Come to meet you. Jennifer's been held up at Inverloss. Something about the boiler. She gave me a ring and asked me to come and collect you." He stood there, looking down at her. "Do I get a kiss?"
Claudia reached up and planted a peck on his cold cheek. "I didn't know you'd be around."
"Oh, yes, I'm around. A local inhabitant now. Is this all your luggage?" He swept it up. "Come along now."
She followed him, almost running to keep up with his long legs, through the gate and out into the station yard where a large and battered estate car awaited them. A dog looked out of the back window. Its nose had made smeary marks on the glass. Magnus flung open the boot and tossed Claudia's suitcase in with the dog, and then came around to open the front door for her. She got in. The car smelt of dog and the inside looked as though it hadn't been cleaned out for months, but Magnus made

unverwüstlich • wettergegerbt

ihn mit offenem Mund anstarrte

abzuholen • hat mich angerufen • abzuholen • reckte sich • gab ihm ein Küsschen auf die ... Wange • hob es schwungvoll hoch • Kombi

Kofferraum

entschuldigte sich nicht

- [ ] However she was pretty surprised when she saw who was waiting for her.
- [ ] In the course of their conversation they established that the lady knew Jennifer.
- [ ] Magnus had changed but she still recognised him, even after all these years.
- [ ] At their destination the lady was picked up by her husband, the shepherd, but there was no sign of Jennifer.
- [ ] She told her that she had visited her sister and done some shopping.

no apologies as he settled himself beside her, slammed the door and started up the engine. Gravel shot from behind the back wheels and they were away. She remembered that he had never been a man to waste time.

She said, "But what do you do here?"

"I run my father's old woollen mill."

"But you always swore you'd never do that. You were going to be independent, go out on your own."

"And so I was for a bit. Worked in the Borders* and then Yorkshire. Then I went to Germany for a couple of years and ended up in New York as a wool broker. But then my father died, and the mill started running down and was going to be sold, so I came home."

There was an air of tremendous confidence about him. She said, and it was a statement and not a question, "And pulled it all together."

"Tried to. At least we're out of the red now and we've got some important orders coming in. Doubled the workforce. You must come and see it. See if you approve of our end product."

"And what is that?"

"Tweeds, but much finer than the ones my father used to make. Closer weaves, lighter weights. Hard-wear-

den Motor anließ

leite • Wollspinnerei

Wollhändler • mit der Spinnerei ging es bergab • er strahlte ... aus • hast das Ruder herumgerissen • habe ... verdoppelt • Belegschaft • dichter • Gewebe • strapazierfähig

info

Die Borders sind ein Verwaltungsbezirk im Süden Schottlands, sie bilden einen Teil des Grenzlands zu England.

**Übung 37** Diese Wörter haben mehrere Bedeutungen. Kreuzen Sie die richtigen an.

| | | | |
|---|---|---|---|
| **1.** statement | ☐ Aussage | ☐ Staat | ☐ Bankauszug |
| **2.** close | ☐ nah | ☐ schwül | ☐ eng |
| **3.** air | ☐ Luft | ☐ Ausstrahlung | ☐ Melodie |
| **4.** to run | ☐ rinnen | ☐ rennen | ☐ leiten |

ing, but not hard. Malleable, I think the word is. And some amazing colours."

anschmiegsam

"Are you designing?"

"Yes."

"And where are the important orders coming from?"

"All over the world."

"That's marvellous. And where do you live?"

"In Pa's old house."

Old Mr Ballater's house. Claudia remembered it, built high on the hill above the town. It had a large garden and a tennis court. Many energetic afternoons had been spent there, for Magnus, a year or so older than Claudia and Jennifer, had been one of a pack of youngsters who had spent all their time together. Leaving school, he had studied textile design and that last summer of all he was already a first-year student.

aktiv

Horde

in jenem letzten Sommer • studierte ... im ersten Semester

That had been a special summer for a number of reasons. The weather was one of them, for it had been exceptionally warm and dry and the long, light northern evenings had seen many fishing expeditions, walks up the river bank and quiet hours spent casting for trout. The social life was another. They were all grown up now, and never had there been such an endless round of picnics and golf matches and tennis tournaments and reel parties and midnight barbecues on the beach. But Magnus, perhaps, had been the most important reason of all, for his enormous energy and his appetite for new diversions had swept them all up in his wake. A young man who never tired, was never bored nor out of humour, who owned his own car, and generally gave the impression that never for one moment did he doubt that life was for living and every day to be filled with enjoyment.

sie alle mitgerissen • schlechte Laune

"But tell me about yourself." Driving at an alarming rate, they were already through the little town and out into the countryside beyond. "Jennifer says you haven't been north for twenty years. How could you stay out of touch for so long?"

beunruhigend schnell

nichts von dir hören lassen

"We weren't out of touch. We've always written to each other and telephoned, and every now and then Jennifer comes to London for a day or two and stays with me and we go shopping and to the theatre …"

"But twenty years. So long since we were all together. What times those were." He turned to smile at her, and Claudia prayed that a car was not bombing towards them around the curve of the road. "Why didn't you come? Were you too busy?"

entgegenraste

"Like you. Learning a trade. Getting experience. Starting a business."

Ich habe einen Beruf erlernt.

"Interior designing. Jennifer told me. Where do you operate?"

arbeitest

"London. The King's Road*. I've got a shop and my own workrooms. Lots of commissions; too many, sometimes."

Werkstatt • Aufträge

"Who runs it while you're away?"

"I have an assistant."

"You sound successful."

Claudia thought about this. "I suppose I am."

His eyes were back on the road. He said, "You never married?"

"I suppose Jennifer told you that, as well."

**info** Die King's Road gehört zu den schicksten Einkaufsstraßen Londons. Sie führt durch den Stadtteil Chelsea.

**Übung 38** Finden Sie das jeweilige Synonym zu den angegebenen Wörtern. Viel Spaß beim Rätseln!

| **Down** (senkrecht) | **Across** (waagerecht) |
|---|---|
| **1** embarrassed | **3** quietly |
| **2** difficult | **4** profession |
| | **5** order |

"Of course. I found it hard to believe."

Claudia knew a stirring of feminine irritation. Her voice was cool. "I suppose you imagined that my only potential was a house, a husband and children?"

wurde bewusst, dass die Frau in ihr sich ärgerte

"No," Magnus replied calmly, "I didn't imagine anything of the sort. I was just surprised that a girl so beautiful hadn't been snapped up years ago."

nicht schon ... weggeschnappt worden ist

He spoke so naturally, so reasonably, that Claudia was ashamed of her own thoughtless words. She said, "I'm doing what I want to do," but thought of Giles, and then did not think of Giles because Giles was in America and this place and this moment and this man beside her had no part of Giles. "I am being independent."

"May I say that it suits you?"

She was touched. "Yes, I should like that very much." She smiled, and smoothly changed the direction of the conversation. "And you, Magnus? A wife?"

"Still unresolved."

"What does that mean?"

"That I never actually gathered up the courage to make the great commitment. A certain amount of dabbling has taken place, of course, but not the dreaded plunge."

Once more he turned his head to look into her face,

ungeklärt • mich ernsthaft zu binden • Rumprobieren • Sprung ins kalte Wasser

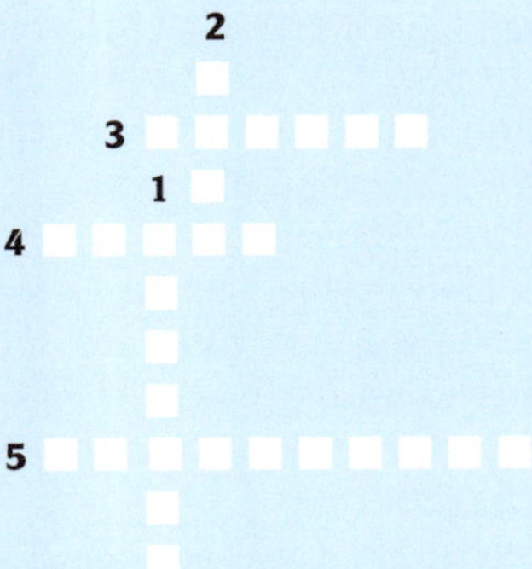

and his blue eyes gleamed with amusement. "It would appear that we are birds of a feather."

Claudia turned away, made no comment. She knew that he was mistaken, and they were not birds of a feather, but she was not going to tell him so. *A certain amount of dabbling has taken place.* It was not difficult to imagine the extent of these dabbling for he was, and always had been, an extremely attractive man. But she had not dabbled. Since meeting Giles eight years ago she had remained constant to him; seen him through an unsatisfactory marriage and an acrimonious divorce and, staunchly, been around ever since. And Magnus's dreaded plunge, the final commitment of marriage, she did not fear, but longed for.

Inverloss lay back from the road, reached by a rutted track and sheltered by a stand of ancient beeches and oaks. Bumping down the lane, Claudia looked for change and was grateful to see little. A new barn had been built, and there was a cattle grid between the road and the garden, but otherwise all was just the same. Beyond the cattle grid, sea pebbles did duty as gravel and approaching the house had always sounded just like driving across a beach. Magnus put the heel of his hand on the horn in a long blast, and before Claudia could open the door of the car Jennifer was there, erupting out of the house with dogs at her heels and a toddler on her hip. She wore jeans and a sweatshirt, her freckled face shone with good health, her hair was a curly mop, and she looked no different from the tomboy teenager she had once been.

"Oh, Jennifer ..."

Jennifer set the toddler down and they hugged. All the dogs, including Magnus's, began to bark, and the child's face crumpled and he began to howl, so Jennifer picked him up again and he gazed at Claudia with baleful, tear-brimmed eyes.

"I'm sorry I couldn't get to meet you but Ronnie's fishing, and the man came to see about the boiler.

funkelten vor • vom gleichen Schlag sind

war sie ihm treu geblieben • hatte ihm über ... hinweggeholfen • bitter • unerschütterlich • ausgefahren • während sie ... entlangrumpelten • Weidenrost

Handballen • Hupe • Tuten

Kleinkind • sommersprossig

jungenhaft

verzog sich • brüllen • böse • in Tränen schwimmend

We've been waiting for days and he had to come on a Saturday!"
"No problem. I'm here."
"Magnus, you are a saint. Stay and have lunch with us. It's such a gorgeous day, we're going to go blackberrying. We decided this morning that this is going to be our blackberry day. Jane and Rory are riding their ponies but they'll be back soon."
There had always, every year, as far back as Claudia could remember, been a blackberry day. A traditional expedition to pick the dark fruit for a twelve month's supply of jellies and jams.
She said, "Are we going to Creagan Hill?"
"But of course. Where else? Do come, Magnus. We can always do with an extra pair of hands."
"All right. But I have to go back to the mill first – there are a few things I have to sort out. What time's lunch?"
"Around one."
"I'll be there."

The inside of the house was no different. Such comfort. It smelt the same, a bit musky and smoky and

saint: Engel • blackberrying: Brombeeren pflücken • jellies: Gelees • I have to sort out: um die ich mich kümmern muss • Such comfort.: So tröstlich. • musky: moschusartig • smoky: rauchig

**Übung 39**

Was bedeuten die folgenden Ausdrücke? Kreuzen Sie die richtige Antwort an.

**1.** a twelve month's supply of jellies and jams
- ☐ jellies and jams to sell for a year
- ☐ enough jellies and jams to last a year

**2.** I have to sort out a few things.
- ☐ I have to take care of a few things.
- ☐ I have to get rid of a few things.

torfig • Schmutzflecken

peaty, and there were worn bits on the carpets and grubby marks on the wallpaper, just the height of children's hands.

Kumpel

"Isn't it great that Magnus has come back to Lossdale to live? It's like old times. He and Ronnie are tremendous buddies, and he's doing wonders at the mill. Were you surprised to see him?"

Jennifer, hefting her baby, led the way upstairs and Claudia, carrying her suitcase, followed. Across the wide landing, then Jennifer flung open a door and walked into the sunlight beyond.

Bettdecken • Schrankkoffer • Dachboden • Reiseklamotten • tapsend • Kommode • plumpste auf • Hosenboden • Messinggriffe • Schatz

"I put you in here, it's the room you always had." Claudia went to lay her suitcase on the seat of a chair. "Don't you adore the new bedspreads? I found them in a trunk in the attic. You must be longing to get out of your trainy clothes. I can't wait to introduce you to Ronnie. I can't believe you've never met him! And Jane and Rory. This one's called Geordie." She set him on his feet and sat herself down on the edge of the bed. Geordie, tottering slightly, made his way to the chest of drawers, thumped down on his bottom and began to play with one of the brass handles. "He's such a love." Claudia was at the window, standing with her back to

**Übung 40** In diesem Text sind acht inhaltliche Fehler versteckt. Streichen Sie sie an.

It was hard to believe but Claudia had never met Jennifer's children, Ronnie, Jane, Rory and Geordie, before. Jennifer was thrilled Claudia would finally get to know them. She was also excited and keen to show Claudia all the new things in the flat, among them the bedspreads that she had discovered in a wooden chest in the attic. She was a little envious though that Claudia was so independent and successful and had such stylish clothes. She also admired Claudia for being so slim. However she was aware of Claudia's unsteady relationship with Giles whom she had met

her cousin, looking down over the fields to the distant sea. She said, "I was so afraid everything would be changed, but it isn't." She turned back to smile at Jennifer. "Nor have you. You never do."

"You've changed," said Jennifer bluntly. "You've lost weight. You're dreadfully thin."

"That's just London. And we're both thirty-seven now. Not girls any longer."

"I didn't say you looked old. Just thin. And sort of polished." Jennifer's gaze was steady and unblinking. "Why did you suddenly decide to come, at a day's notice? Or don't you want to talk about it?" There had never been secrets between them. Claudia lowered her head and began to unbutton the jacket of her suit. "It's Giles, isn't it?"

And it was a relief to have her say his name; to have it said so that it did not have to hang, like a spectre, between them.

Jennifer knew about Giles. Had gleaned what she could from letters, and had met him once in London when Giles had taken the pair of them out for dinner. At that time he had been divorced for nearly a year. "Is he going to marry you?" Jennifer had asked, but Claudia

geradeheraus

glänzend • unverwandt • von einem Tag auf den anderen

Gespenst

aus ... entnommen

once when she was visiting her in London. They had never been very open with each other so she carefully quizzed Claudia about her surprise visit. She realised though that she might not tell her what was really going on.

had laughed and told her that it was not like that at all, they were simply good friends.

Giles. Handsome, successful, charming, but paranoiacally elusive. He and Claudia each kept their separate establishments but they were lovers. They were a pair, accepted as a couple and, when asked away for country weekends, went together and stayed together.

But Giles's job as a money-broker was far-reaching. Much of his time he spent in New York where he had an apartment in the city, and often he was away for three or four months at a time. She did not know when he was returning until he called her. "I am back," he would say. "I am here." Whereupon, as if their separation had never taken place, the pattern of a shared life was taken up again: the dinner party in Giles's house which Claudia was glad to organise; the contacting of mutual friends; the intimate evenings in their favourite Italian restaurant; the magic nights, their love shared in Claudia's huge, downy bed.

And life changed colour and became vital, with energies to spare so that the day-to-day demands of home and job and business presented no problems, rather, were a challenge which Claudia gladly met.

paranoisch • ausweichend • Wohnungen

Finanzmakler • brachte viele Reisen mit sich

gemeinsam • daunenweich • lebendig • voll überschüssiger Energie • Anforderungen • Herausforderung, der sich ... stellte • gerne

**info**

Die Konstruktion would + Verb wird auch verwendet, wenn man ausdrücken will, dass Dinge bisher oder in der Vergangenheit oft oder immer getan wurden oder passiert sind. Giles would say "I am back." – das heißt, er verschwand oft monateweise, meldete sich dann bei Claudia und sagte meist „Ich bin wieder da."

She felt fulfilled, each tomorrow bright with promise. So much so that it was hard to believe that it was not the same for Giles. One day, she told herself, tomorrow he will discover that he cannot exist without me. But then that tomorrow would bring a telephone call to let her know that Giles was once more on his way, his flight dictated by the vagaries of his job. And he would be gone, across the Atlantic, leaving her alone to get on as best she could with her single, lonely existence.

Wechselfällen

Jennifer was waiting. Claudia said, at last, "Yes, it's Giles. We were going to Spain with a party of friends. Everything booked. But he's been held up in New York and we had to cancel. I could have gone, but it would have been pointless on my own."

Gruppe von Freunden

sinnlos

"How long has he been away this time?"

"A few months. He was due back three days ago."

sollte ... zurückkommen

"How mean."

Claudia sprang to Giles's defence. "It's not his fault."

"You make excuses for him. Does he ever write to you? Is he ever in touch?"

"He telephones. Sometimes. He's a busy man."

"More excuses. I suppose you love him. Would you marry him?"

"I ..." Claudia sought for the right words. "Yes. Yes, I do. I mean, I want to be married. I want to have children. Everybody thinks I'm a dedicated career woman, but I would love to have children. Soon I'll be too old."

"Are you certain," Jennifer asked with disconcerting frankness, "that you are not simply his London lady?"

The feared, unacknowledged suspicion. As she had always done, Claudia shrugged it away. "There's a possibility, I suppose."

mit Leib und Seele • irritierend • Offenheit • befürchtet • uneingestanden

"Do you trust him?"

"I don't think about trust."

"But Claudia, trust is the most important thing of all. Don't waste your life."

"How could I walk away from Giles? It's too big a

verlassen

Das packe ich nicht. • Lass los. • durch … erschüttert • schrill • Turnschuhe • eingerahmt

decision. I can't handle it. He's part of me now, I've loved him for too long."

"Yes. Too long. Cut loose."

Claudia said, "I can't."

They fell silent. This silence was shattered by doors opening and slamming shut, footsteps, high-pitched voices calling up the stairs. "Mummy! We're back. We're starving!"

Jennifer sighed. She got to her feet and went to gather Geordie up into her arms. She said, "I must go and see to lunch. We'll talk some more."

She went. Claudia alone, unpacked and changed into old jeans and trainers. She cleaned her face, brushed her hair. As she did this she heard a car drawing up outside the front door and, looking from the window, saw Magnus, returned from his mill.

He got out of the car and started towards the house. Claudia watched him but, as though she had called out his name, he suddenly stopped and looked up and saw her there, framed in the upstairs window.

He said, "Are you not ready, yet, for lunch?"

"Yes, I'm ready. On my way."

**Übung 41** Vervollständigen Sie die Verben, beziehungsweise Ausdrücke, indem Sie Linien ziehen.

| | |
|---|---|
| to slam | up |
| to see to | loose |
| to cut | out |
| to gather | lunch |
| to call | shut |

Creagan Hill lay three miles from Inverloss on the far side of the little town. From a rounded summit, crowned with scree and rock, it swept down, heather-clad, to the coastal plain, there giving way to a scattering of small drystone-dyked fields where bracken grew and sheep grazed. Narrow lanes wound around the margins of these fields, sheltered from the prevailing wind and in the full face of the sun. Here were the bramble thickets and the fat, dark blackberries clustered, ripening, upon the thorny stems.
The prospect of the expedition filled Jennifer's children with unsophisticated anticipation.
"We go every year," Jane explained through a mouthful of cottage pie. "And we get absolutely filthy, and the person who's picked the most gets a prize. I got it last year …"
"You stole some of mine," Rory pointed out. He was a stolid child, with blue eyes and his mother's hair.
"I didn't, you gave them to me."
"I'd filled my bucket. I didn't have any more room."
Magnus tactfully intervened. "Never mind. Perhaps this year everybody will get a prize."
"Even Geordie?"

Gipfel • Geröll • fiel … sanft ab • heidekrautbewachsen • vereinzelt • von Trockensteinmauern umrahmt • Adlerfarn • weideten • Brombeerdickichte • hingen in Trauben • Aussicht auf • schlicht • Vorfreude • Hackfleischauflauf • dreckig • phlegmatisch

**Übung 42**

Ordnen Sie das Wirrwarr und finden Sie jeweils ein Wort und sein Gegenteil.

| | |
|---|---|
| filthy | pointed |
| wide | perhaps |
| stolid | rounded |
| clean | energetic |
| definitely | narrow |

"Why not?"

"He'll just be a nuisance and get under everybody's feet, and eat berries. He'll probably make himself sick."

Geordie banged a spoon on his highchair and, when they all looked at him, dissolved into delighted laughter.

geht allen … auf die Nerven • nur • Ihm wird … schlecht. • schlug mit einem Löffel gegen • brach in … aus

"In fact," Jennifer said, when they had all stopped laughing at Geordie, "Jane's got a point. Geordie certainly won't last the whole afternoon. So I think we should take two cars and then I can bring him home when he starts to flag."

hat recht • durchhalten • müde … werden

"I want to go with Magnus," Jane announced. "I'm going in his car."

Rory was not to be outdone. "Me, too."

wollte nicht zurückstehen

Their mother sighed. "I don't mind who goes with who, but how about getting the plates into the dishwasher and then we can make a start?"

And so Claudia found herself once more seated beside Magnus in his car, with Rory and Jane on the back seat and Magnus's dog in the boot. The expression on the dog's face was long-suffering and Claudia did not blame him. Jennifer went ahead, the baby strapped into his chair behind her, and Magnus, at a more prudent speed than their drive that morning, brought up the rear of the little procession.

die eines schwer geprüften • fuhr vor • umsichtig • bildete die Nachhut

The afternoon fulfilled the promise of the early morning and remained incredibly bright, clear and warm. Once they left the town behind them Claudia saw the shape of the hills, the brilliance of the sea. Sunlight streamed down over tawny bracken and the plum-bloom of the heather. They turned off the road and plunged into a maze of small lanes heading away from the sea, and Creagan Hill reared up before them so steeply that the summit was lost from view.

goldbraun • lila blühend • Gewirr

Rory and Jane were asking riddles.

"What's green and goes at a hundred miles an hour?"

gaben Rätsel auf • fährt

"A ton-up gooseberry."
"Why did the razorbill raise 'er bill?"
"Because she wanted the sea urchin to see 'er chin. Get it, Rory? See 'er chin."
Screams of laughter.
Claudia opened her window and let the wind blow in on her face. It was cold and smelt of grass and moss and seaweed, and she thought of Spain and was, quite suddenly, glad that she was here and not there.
They reached the chosen spot at last, spilled out of the cars and set to work. Ranged along the roadside, scrambling over dykes into the fields, they picked busily all afternoon. The plastic buckets were slowly filled. Mouths and fingers were stained purple, sweaters snagged, jeans torn, shoes coated with mud. By four o'clock little Geordie had had enough and Jennifer decided that it was time to take him home.
"He's been so good, sitting in that nice bit of bog and looking for ladybirds, haven't you, my poppet?" She kissed his filthy face. "Anyway, I've got to get back and do something about dinner. Come and eat dinner with us, Magnus."
"You've already fed me."

die 100 Meilen pro Stunde fährt • Stachelbeere • Tordalk • = her • Schnabel • Seeigel • Moos • Seetang

verteilt • kletterten sie über • Mauer • waren ... verfärbt • hatten Fäden gezogen • waren verdreckt mit • Matsch • Sumpf • Marienkäfer • Schätzchen

bewirtet

**Übung 43**

In jeder Reihe steht ein Wort oder Name, das oder der nicht zu den anderen passt. Streichen Sie ihn durch.

**1.** razorbill – seaweed – ladybird – sea urchin
**2.** mud – laughter – window – moss
**3.** Rory – Jennifer – Magnus – Claudia
**4.** to kiss – to feed – to eat – to smell

"We'll feed you again. No problem. And Ronnie will want to tell you all about the fish he didn't catch. Who's coming with me?"

Jane and Rory debated and finally decided to go with their mother. They were sated with blackberries and there was a television programme they wanted to watch.

hatten sich an … satt gegessen

"How about you two?"

Claudia put her heavy bucket of berries into the boot of Jennifer's car and stretched her aching arms and shoulders. "It's such a beautiful day, I can't bear to waste a moment of it." She looked at Magnus. "Perhaps we could take your dog for a walk? So far, he seems to have had a fairly boring day."

Magnus agreed. "Whatever. We could climb the hill and look at the view. Would you like that?"

It was exactly what she had been wanting to do all afternoon. She said, "Yes, I'd love it."

Jennifer departed, the children waving from the open windows of the car as though they were saying good-bye for ever. When they were gone, Magnus turned to Claudia.

**Übung 44** Welche Sätze gehören zusammen? Tragen Sie den entsprechenden Buchstaben in die Kästchen ein.

**1.** ☐ It was such a beautiful day.
**2.** ☐ The dog was happy.
**3.** ☐ Magnus suggested climbing the hill.
**4.** ☐ The children went home with their mother.
**5.** ☐ The turf was firm.

"So. What are we waiting for?"

They set off. Up through the fields, up the gradually steepening slope; through broken gateways and knee-high bracken and on, up again, until they were surrounded by heather. The dog, delighted at last to have some attention paid to it, raced ahead, scenting rabbits, his great tail plumbing. A few old sheep, seeing them approach, ceased their grazing and stared. Now Claudia could feel the wind on her cheeks and was grateful for its coolness, and was grateful too for the path which stretched ahead, for the firmness of the close-cropped turf, which made for pleasant walking. She could feel the stretch and pull of the muscles in her legs, and her lungs were filled with air as pure and as cold as fresh spring water.

steiler werdend • kaputt • Tore • hocherfreut, dass • ihn ... jemand beachtete • witterte • stand senkrecht • hörten auf zu grasen • kurz geschnitten • Gras

About halfway up the hill they came upon a grassy corrie cleft by a tiny burn, miniature waterfalls bubbling down over a bed of white pebbles. Claudia was thirsty. She knelt and scooped water up in her palm and drank it. It tasted of peat. She sat then, with her back to the hill and her eyes, for the first time, turned upon the view.

grasbewachsen • Kar • den ... durchschnitt • Bach

"I had no idea that we had come so far, and climbed so high."

**a)** That was exactly what Claudia had wanted to do.
**b)** They wanted to watch a TV programme.
**c)** It was pleasant to walk on it.
**d)** Claudia couldn't bear to waste a moment of it.
**e)** Finally someone paid attention to it.

"You've done well." He settled himself beside her, his knees drawn up. He shaded his eyes with his hand. "No need to climb further. We won't get a better sighting than this."

angezogen

He was right. A spectacular view, remembered from years back, but always breathtaking. It took in the curve of the coastline, the fields and the farms and the inland lochs. All was spread before them like some giant-sized map. So clear was the air that the mountains, some fifty miles to the south, showed themselves, their peaks frosted with the first snows of the winter. And ahead was the sea, on this day blue as the Mediterranean, the wine-dark seas of Homer's Greece. And the silence. Only the wind, the song of a lark, the long, sad call of a curlew. Sitting still, they were soon chilled by the wind. Claudia, who had taken off her sweater and tied the arms around her waist, now undid the knot and pulled the sweater on again.

umfasste

riesig

tintenschwarz

Brachvogel •

fröstelten ... durch den Wind

• Ärmel

He said, "You mustn't get cold."

"I'm all right. And it's good for the soul just to look at a view like that on a day like today. How fortunate we are. You in particular, because now you live here all the time."

**Übung 45** Ergänzen Sie die Wörter aus den folgenden Wortfamilien, die auch auf dieser Doppelseite zu finden sind.

| noun | verb | adjective |
|---|---|---|
| length | | long |
| frost | to frost | |
| shade | to shade | |
| chill | | chilly |
| breath | | breathtaking |

"I know what you mean. It gets everything into proportion."
"It makes me feel like an ant."
"An ant?"
"Tiny. Insignificant. Unimportant."
But not just herself. All of life, with its problems: working, making money, loving. Being up here, so high above the world, was like seeing the day-to-day rat-race through the wrong end of a telescope so that all became diminished, weightless and trivial. And if Claudia were an ant, then the Atlantic was no more than a pond, and New York a dot on the globe, yet alive with the millions of teeming insects which peopled that teeming glut of humanity. Giles was one of them.
Magnus spoke. He said, "Would you actually want to live here all the time?"
"I've never thought about it. But here is Jennifer, so happy. With her husband and her farm and her children. Yet I don't suppose it would ever do for me."
"Life is strange. All of us scattered all over the place, and then after all these years … Why should you and I, of all people, find ourselves here and now, halfway up Creagan Hill and on a God-given day, to boot?"
"I have no idea, Magnus."
He said, "I wonder if you have any idea of how much I was in love with you?"
Claudia, frowning, turned to gaze at him in total puzzlement. His profile was sombre. She could see the lines around his mouth, the crow's feet, the strands of grey in his thick, dark hair. Then he turned and looked into her face, and she saw his eyes, and for once there was no laughter in them.
She said, "You can't be serious."
"You had no idea?"
"I was seventeen."
"You were amazing. So beautiful that I was scared of

Konkurrenzkampf • klein wurde • unbedeutend • Teich • Punkt • Gewimmel von Millionen von Insekten • bevölkerten • wuselnde Schwemme der Menschheit • mir … genügen

Bilderbuchtag • obendrein

völlig verblüfft

Krähenfüße • graue Strähnen

unerreichbar — how I felt because I was so certain that you were unattainable."

"You never said ..."

"Nor let it show."

"But why? Why not?"

"It wasn't the time. We were too young. Scarcely out of school, with all our lives in front of us. Everything to be learned, to be done. The world our oyster, filled with people waiting to love. And all we wanted was to get out and discover it for ourselves.

die Welt stand uns offen

I had a photograph of you. I used to carry it round and show it to my mates. 'This is my first love,' I would say. I didn't say, 'my only love'. That's what I should have said."

Kumpel

"Why do you tell me now?"

"Because I am too old for pride."

Simply spoken. Claudia dropped her eyes, not wishing him to read her thoughts. I am too old for pride as well, but I've hung on to it because, as far as Giles is concerned, it seems to be the only way I can hold on to him. Bleak knowledge. She thought about opening her heart to Magnus and telling him about Giles – explaining, trying to make him understand – but knew that

senkte den Blick

daran festgehalten

**Übung 46** Ergänzen Sie die Lücken mit dem jeweils passenden Wort aus der Klammer. (pride, pain, unload, state of mind, comfort, mates, oyster)

**1.** Magnus used to tell his ____________________ that Claudia was his first love.

**2.** When they were young they had all their lives in front of them – the world was their ____________________.

**3.** Just like Magnus, Claudia thought she was too old for ____________________.

she could never inflict such pain. Not now, not while she was in such a confused and distressed state of mind. Giles was her life and her love but also her problem, and not one to be unloaded on to this man, this old friend, who had just declared his own undying love for her.

No. It must be kept inconsequent, light-hearted. She smiled. She said, "Pride is a nuisance anyway. It just gets between people."

"Yes. And then you say nothing until it is too late. Better perhaps, not to say anything at all."

"Don't feel like that." The afternoon was dying, the sun sinking behind them, the last of its rays casting long shadows. The wind, rising, bent the long grasses which grew on the banks of the little burn. Claudia shivered. She said, "It's getting cold," and then, because he looked so much in need of comfort, she leaned forward and kissed his mouth. "It's time we went home, Magnus."

After that it was all right again. He grinned, ruefully, but still it was a smile of sorts, and got to his feet. He held out a hand to help Claudia up, whistled for his dog and they set off. The downward slope was easy going

zufügen • bekümmert • Verfassung
unsterblich
belanglos • unbekümmert
Strahlen
voll Bedauern • eine Art

**4.** Claudia didn't want to cause Magnus any ____________________ by telling him about Giles.

**5.** Magnus looked as if he needed someone to ____________________ him.

**6.** Claudia didn't want to ____________________ her problems on to Magnus after he had confessed that she was his only love.

**7.** Her ____________________ was one of confusion and distress.

and, by the time they reached the car, he was his old, cheerful self again, and full of plans for the evening ahead.

"... I must buy some wine for Ronnie. Do you mind if we stop off in the town for a moment while I do a quick bit of shopping? I'm out of bacon, as well, and I need a bag of dog biscuits."

In the last golden light of the afternoon, the main street of Inverloss bustled with the last activities of the day. The shops were still open: the butcher, the greengrocer, the fishing-tackle shop. The Italian café spilled neon light out on to the pavement, and from its interior came the sound of pop music and the evocative smell of frying fish and chips. Girls hung around outside the café, giggling in their Saturday finery, tight jeans and earrings, and the young men sat across the road, outside the pub, and eyed them.

Magnus drew up by the newsagent. "I won't be long."

He disappeared into the shop and emerged almost immediately with a newspaper. Through the open window, he dropped it on to her lap. "This'll keep you amused."

He strode off.

It was this morning's paper he had brought her, a national tabloid printed in London. She cast her eye over the screaming headlines and then slowly scanned the rest of the paper, glancing at items, photographs, advertisements. She turned to the Social Diary and saw the picture of Giles.

It was neither a very large nor a very good photograph, but it leapt at her as a known name will leap from a column of newsprint. He stood with a girl on his arm. A fair-haired girl with a long cascade of hair. She wore a low-necked dress; her arms were bare. She carried a small bunch of flowers. Giles was smiling, showing his teeth. He looked overweight, a bit ponderous. He was sporting a tremendously spotted tie.

habe keinen ... mehr • Hundekuchen • auf ... herrschte ein reges Treiben mit • Gemüsehändler • Laden für Angelbedarf • Erinnerungen wachrufend • brutzelnd • Ausgehkleidung

überregional • Boulevardzeitung • sensationsheischend • Schlagzeilen • Gesellschaftsseite • sprang ... entgegen • Zeitungsspalte • langem, wallendem Haar • tief ausgeschnitten • nackt • schwerfällig • hatte ... an • stark getüpfelt

The caption: 'Giles Savours with his young bride, Debbie Peyton. See column four.' — Bildunterschrift

Her first instinctive thought was, 'It can't be true. It's a ghastly mistake. They've got it all wrong.' Quite suddenly she felt dreadfully cold, her lips frozen, her mouth dry. 'It can't be true.'

Column four.

The headline in thick black type: 'BUSINESS AS USUAL FOR GILES AND DEBBIE'. And then the story: — Schrift

There will be no immediate honeymoon for London businessman Giles Savours (44) who was married this week in the Church of St Michael, Brewsville, New York State. Giles, a partner with the City firm Wolfson-Rilke, has work aplenty to keep him at his desk in his New York office, but plans to jet to Barbados for Christmas. — haufenweise

His lovely bride Debbie Peyton (22) is the only daughter of Charlie D. Peyton of Consolidated Aluminium. A petite 5'2", she met Savours for the first time only three months ago, but their whirlwind courtship has not gone unobserved by Giles's New York colleagues. This is his second time around – his previous wife was — zierlich • 1,55 m (= 5 feet 2 inches) • stürmisch • Romanze • zweiter Anlauf

**Übung 47**

Sind die folgenden Aussagen wahr oder falsch? Tragen Sie ein T für true oder ein F für false in die Kästchen ein.

**1.** ☐ Claudia fainted when she read the headlines in the Social Diary of the paper.

**2.** ☐ Giles had not even had the decency to let Claudia know that he was getting married.

**3.** ☐ Giles had known his bride for more than a year.

**4.** ☐ Magnus didn't realise what he would trigger by buying the paper.

**5.** ☐ Claudia had fooled herself into believing that she had a future with Giles.

Lady Priscilla Rolands – and his friends were beginning to doubt if he would ever take the plunge again …

She could not read any more. The light was too dim, the newsprint wavered, the words blurred together. Giles, married. She thought of his voice over the transatlantic telephone lines, easy as ever, ripe with reasonable excuses. "Terribly sorry. Something's come up. No possibility of my getting back to London in time for Spain. I know you'll understand. Why don't you go without me? You'll have a great time … Yes, of course … Just as soon as I can …"

And so on. The same voice, the same old let-down. Nothing new. Except this time he hadn't even had the courage to tell her that he was going to be married to another woman. A girl. Young enough to be his daughter. He was married. Gone from Claudia. It was over.

She still felt numb with cold. She thought, 'I am numb with shock.' She sat in Magnus's car and waited for her reactions to make themselves evident. For rage. Perhaps screams of fury. For furious tears of rank humiliation. For a terrible sense of loss. But none of these

Druckerschwärze • verschwammen • unbefangen • voll von

Enttäuschung

war …

taub vor • zum Vorschein kamen • Zorn • Wutschreie • absolut • Demütigung

**Übung 48** Finden Sie die in diesem Buchstabendickicht versteckten acht Wörter. Sie sind senkrecht (von oben nach unten), waagerecht (von links nach rechts) und diagonal (von links oben nach rechts unten angeordnet).

Die deutschen Entsprechungen der Wörter lauten

| | |
|---|---|
| Entschuldigung | Erleichterung |
| taub | Schrei |
| Steuerrad | Beere |
| Süßigkeiten | Stimme |

things happened and, after a bit, she realised that they would not.

Instead, she discovered that she was experiencing the most unexpected emotions of all. Relief, and a sort of gratitude. Relief because all decisions had been taken out of her hands, and gratitude because perhaps this was the last and the best thing that Giles could have done for her.

gratitude: Dankbarkeit

"Sorry I've been so long." Magnus was back. He hurled a paper sack of dog meal over on to the back seat and then got in behind the wheel, placing a grocer's carrier bag on the floor between them. Claudia heard the clank of bottles. He slammed the door shut.

dog meal: Hundefutter
clank: Geklirr

"I got the wine and some sweets for the children. I remembered, just in time, I'd promised them all prizes for blackberry-picking …"

Claudia said nothing. She did not turn to look at him, but felt his eyes on her face.

"Claudia?" And then, "Is something wrong?"

After a bit, she shook her head.

"Something is wrong."

She stared at the newspaper. Gently, he reached over and took it from her. "What is it?"

| | | | | | | | | | | | |
|---|---|---|---|---|---|---|---|---|---|---|---|
| l | p | t | b | e | r | r | y | x | z | q | r |
| n | o | b | u | s | t | l | e | q | w | z | e |
| r | v | o | i | c | e | k | s | t | o | t | l |
| g | d | n | n | s | y | e | r | v | b | l | i |
| v | i | e | u | m | t | v | w | e | d | l | e |
| e | s | c | m | k | i | t | p | h | w | z | f |
| x | a | k | b | i | n | s | i | r | e | t | l |
| c | k | l | s | l | y | f | w | y | i | e | i |
| u | l | i | f | v | e | z | j | e | i | n | l |
| s | c | r | e | a | m | s | j | x | e | g | t |
| e | b | e | i | w | e | n | i | m | l | t | r |
| x | y | f | h | p | v | c | o | l | w | l | s |

"Just a man I know."

"What's happened to him?" He obviously feared the worst.

"He's not dead or anything. Just married."

"This guy here? Giles Savours?"

Claudia nodded.

"An old friend?"

"Yes."

"A lover?"

"Yes."

"How long have you known him?"

"Eight years."

verdammt
etwas Nettes

A long pause while Magnus read what Claudia had already read. "Why are ages and measurements always so vital on these bloody pages?" He folded the newspaper with some force and dropped it on the floor. Then he did a kindly thing. He reached out and took her hand in his own. He said, "Do you want to tell me about it?"

machte ... einen Rückzieher

"Nothing to tell. Nothing and everything. It would take too long. But Giles is the reason that I am here. Because we were going to Spain together and he cried off at the last moment. He didn't tell me why, just said that something had come up."

"Didn't you know about this other girl?"

argwöhnisch

"No. I didn't know anything about her. I suppose because I didn't want to know. I wouldn't let myself think about anybody but myself. There is nothing more unattractive than a suspicious woman, and I knew that if I said anything to Giles, what existed between us would all be spoiled."

"That's not much of a basis for a relationship. You deserve better than that."

würdevoller
Zivilcourage

"No. It was my own fault. But it would have been more dignified for both of us had he found the courage to tell me himself. In a way I'm rather sorry for him. It must be dreadful to have so little moral courage."

"I'm not sorry for him. I think he sounds a cruel bastard."

"No. Not cruel, Magnus. One of us had to finish it … it's limped along for long enough. And you mustn't be sorry for me. You think I've been abandoned, but I think I feel as though I've been set free."

Her hand still lay in his. For the first time, she turned her head and looked full into his face, and this time it was he who kissed her.

He said, "It has been, to put it mildly, a remarkable day. And what is more, it is the first day of the rest of your life. So what do you say? Shall we nail our flags to the mast, and make what remains of it just as memorable? After all, we have wine and we have women, and I can always oblige with a song."

Despite everything, she found herself laughing at him. She said, "I'm glad you were the person who was with me. I'm glad that you were the person I was able to tell."

"I'm glad, too," said Magnus.

And that was all. He started up the engine and the car moved forward, down the street and out into the dusky countryside beyond, and Claudia looked out over the sea and saw the moon rising up over the horizon. She felt comforted, and smiled into its silvery face as though she were greeting an old friend.

hört sich wie … an

dahingeplätschert • mir die Freiheit geschenkt worden wäre

unsere Fahnen hissen • denkwürdig • mit … dienen

dämmerig

## Whistle for the Wind

herbeipfeifen

It was Saturday morning. Blinks of golden light lit the trees, and cloud shadows raced across the face of the hills, chasing each other out to the distant blue line of the sea.

Jenny Fairburn, heading home for lunch after a walk with the two family dogs, was pleasantly tired because she had been a long way – right around the loch and back by the rutted, winding farm road. Home lay ahead, an old Manse alongside a ruined church. It was sheltered from the north by a stand of pines, and the south-facing windows flashed in the sunlight as though sending out signals of welcome. Jenny thought about lunch, because she was hungry as well as tired. She knew that it was roast lamb, and her mouth watered, like a hungry child's.

She was, in fact, twenty, a tall, thin girl with the reddish blonde hair and pale skin that she had inherited from her father's mother, a true Highlander. Her eyes were dark, her nose narrow and tip-tilted, and her mouth wide and expressive. When she smiled, it lit up her face, but she knew that when she was feeling cross or depressed she could look sulky and plain.

In the back porch, she gave the panting dogs a drink and then toed off her muddy boots. From the kitchen she could hear her mother's voice, presumably chatting on the telephone, because Jenny's father had spent the morning on the golf-course and his car was still not back in the garage.

In stockinged feet, she let herself into the kitchen, and smelt the roasting lamb and the sharpness of mint sauce.

Blitze • über die Berghänge

ausgefahren • Pfarrhaus • Gruppe

stupsig

wütend war • sah aus, als ob sie beleidigt war • unattraktiv • hechelnd • streifte sich ... ab • in Strümpfen • Schärfe • Minzsoße

"... how very kind of you," her mother was saying. She turned, saw Jenny and smiled in an abstracted way. "Yes. Yes. About six-thirty? All of us. Well, we'll look forward to that. Bye." She put down the receiver and smiled at her daughter. "Did you have a nice walk?"

She sounded a little too bright. Jenny frowned. "Who was that on the telephone?"

Mrs Fairburn was stooping to open the oven door and inspect the lamb. A fragrant gust of heat escaped into the kitchen.

"Just Daphne Fenton."

"What does she want?"

Mrs Fairburn shut the oven door and straightened up. Her face was pink, but perhaps that was just the heat. "She's asked us all for a drink this evening."

"What's the celebration?"

"No celebration. Fergus is home for the weekend, and Daphne's asked a few people in for a drink. She particularly wants you to come."

Jenny said, "I don't want to go."

"Oh, darling, you must."

"You can say I'm doing something else."

Her mother came over to Jenny's side. "Look, I know

receiver – Telefonhörer
bright – fröhlich
was stooping – bückte sich •
fragrant – duftend •
gust – Schwall

**Übung 49** Die folgenden Wörter, die auf dieser Doppelseite vorkommen, haben mehrere Bedeutungen. Kreuzen Sie die richtigen an.

| | | | |
|---|---|---|---|
| **1.** kind | ☐ Sorte | ☐ Kind | ☐ nett |
| **2.** receiver | ☐ Telefonhörer | ☐ Empfänger | ☐ Empfang |
| **3.** bright | ☐ fröhlich | ☐ hell | ☐ klug |
| **4.** battered | ☐ verbeult | ☐ missbraucht | ☐ in Teig gewälzt |
| **5.** to collect | ☐ sammeln | ☐ abholen | ☐ zusammenstellen |

you were hurt, and I know how much you loved Fergus, but it's over. He's marrying Rose next month. At some point you've got to let everybody see that you've accepted this."

"I think I will once they're married. But they're not yet, and I don't like Rose."

They gazed hopelessly at each other, then they heard Mr Faiburn's car coming up the road, turning into the gate.

"There's your father. He'll be starving." Mrs Fairburn gave Jenny's hand a loving pat. "I must make the gravy."

After lunch, with the dishes washed and the kitchen tidy, they dispersed on their various ploys. Mr Fairburn changed into his gardening clothes (in which no self-respecting gardener would be seen dead) and went out to sweep leaves; Mrs Fairburn disappeared to work on the new sitting-room curtains which she had been trying to finish for a month and Jenny decided to go fishing. She collected her rod and her fishing bag, pulled on her father's old shooting jacket and the rubber boots, and firmly told the dogs that this time they couldn't come.

gab Jenny einen ... Klaps auf die Hand • Soße • zerstreuten ... sich mit • Betätigungen • der etwas auf sich hielt

Jagdrock • Gummistiefel

"Is it all right if I borrow your car?" she asked her mother. "I'm going up to the loch to see if I can catch anything."

"Catch at least three trout. Then we can have them for supper."

As Jenny came to the loch, she saw the stillness of the brown water, scarcely touched now by the breeze. 'Too still for fish,' Fergus would have said. 'We'll need to whistle for the wind.'

About a mile down the loch, a grassy track led off the road and down towards the water. Jenny took this, letting the small, battered car bump and bounce its way over tussocks of turf and heather. She parked a few feet from the shore, collected her rod and the bag, and

Büschel • Fuß (1 Fuß = 30,5 cm) • Ufer

made her way down to where the little rowing-boat was pulled up on a sickle of shingle. *kleiner Kiesstrand*

But she didn't get into it at once. Instead, she sat on the bank, and listened to the silence, which was not a silence at all but a stirring and murmuring of tiny sounds. The buzz of a bee, the distant baa-ing of sheep, the sigh of a breeze, the whisper of water against pebbles.

'We'll need to whistle for the wind.'

Fergus ... What could you do about a man who had been part of your life since you were a little girl? A boy in patched jeans, collecting shells on the beach. A young man in a worn kilt, walking the hill. A grown man, immensely sophisticated (*kultiviert*) and attractive, with a smooth dark head and eyes as blue as the loch on a summer day. What could you do about someone with whom you had quarrelled (*mit dem man sich gezankt hatte*) and laughed, who had always been your friend and your rival and finally turned out to be – she knew – the only man she could ever love?

He was six years older than Jenny, which made him now twenty-six, and the son of her parents' friends, the Fentons, who farmed (*bewirtschafteten*) Inverbruie, two miles down the road.

"He's like a brother," people used to say to Jenny who was an only child. But she knew that it had never been like that. For what brother would spend patient hours teaching a small girl how to fish? What brother would dance with a gangling (*schlaksig*) teenager at parties, when the room was filled with older, more charming and prettier girls?

And when Jenny, sent to boarding school (*Internat*) in Kent, hated being away from Scotland so much that every letter home begged to be allowed to return, it was Fergus who eventually persuaded her parents that Jenny would do just as well, and be a thousand times happier, at the local Creagan High School.

'One day,' she had promised herself, 'I shall marry him. He will fall in love with me and I shall marry him, and

I'll move down the road to Inverbruie and be the young farmer's wife.'

But this happy prospect was slightly dimmed by Fergus deciding that he did not want to follow his father into farming, but would go to Edinburgh to learn how to be a chartered accountant.

So what. Jenny's private schemes for the two of them did a quick change of direction. 'One day he will fall in love with me and I shall marry him, and go with him to live in Edinburgh and we'll have a little house in Ann Street and go to symphony concerts together.'

Na und. • eigen • Pläne • wurden schnell abgeändert

The thought of living in Edinburgh was, truth be told, fairly daunting. Jenny hated towns but perhaps Edinburgh wouldn't be too bad. They could come home for weekends.

um ehrlich zu sein • beängstigend

But Fergus did not stay in Edinburgh. After he qualified, he was offered a transfer to the main office of his firm, and moved to London. London? For the first time Jenny knew a nudge of doubt. London. Could she bear to go so far away from her beloved hills and loch?

"Why don't you go to London?" her mother asked when Jenny finally left school. "You could go to college there. Perhaps share a little flat!"

verspürte ... leise Zweifel • mit jemandem eine ... Wohnung teilen

**Übung 50**

Entwirren Sie den Buchstabensalat und ergänzen Sie die Sätze.

**1.** Jenny had known Fergus for ages, they used to both laugh and ____________________. (raqurle)

**2.** Fergus was the one who ____________________ her parents to allow Jenny to leave boarding school and come home. (dudespare)

**3.** Jenny had lots of ____________________ for Fergus' and her future life together. (mechess)

**4.** But Fergus went to Edinburgh and ____________________ as a chartered accountant. (edilafuiq)

"I couldn't bear it. It would be worse than Kent."
"Edinburgh, then? You ought to get away from home for a bit."

Stenografie • erweiterte ihre Französischkenntnisse • wie erwartet • Zeugnis

So Jenny went to Edinburgh and learned shorthand and typing, studied French and went to art galleries, and when she became homesick, climbed Arthur's Seat* and pretended she was on the top of Ben Creagan. By Easter, she had finished the course and been duly presented with a Certificate, and it was time to go home. Fergus would probably be home for Easter as well and she wondered if he would notice a change in her.
He would probably look at her, like people did in books, as though seeing her for the first time, and perhaps then he would recognise what Jenny had known for years. That they were made for each other. And at last all those

unerreichbar

elusive daydreams would come true. It would, of course, mean living in London, but by now Jenny knew that living anywhere without Fergus was no fun at all.

nach ... einfuhr • lehnte ... aus

As her train drew into Creagan, she hung out of the window and saw her mother waiting for her, which was odd, because usually it was her father who met her.
"Darling!" They hugged and kissed, and there was the

**info**

Arthur's Seat ist ein vor 35 Millionen Jahren erloschener Vulkan mitten in Edinburgh, der etwa 250 Meter hoch ist. Er ist ein beliebtes Ziel bei Spaziergängern, man fühlt sich dort, als wäre man mitten im Hochland. Woher der Name kommt, ist ungeklärt – vermutlich hat er nichts mit dem gleichnamigen König Arthur zu tun.

**Übung 51** Auf welche Wörter im Text beziehen sich die folgenden Synonyme?

| | | | | | |
|---|---|---|---|---|---|
| strange | ______ | maybe | ______ | too | ______ |
| realise | ______ | lean out | ______ | normally | ______ |

business of getting cases off the train and making their way out into the yard where the car waited. It was now nearly dark, street lights were on, and the air smelt of hills and peat.

They came through the little town and turned on to the side road which led to home. They passed Inverbruie.

"Is Fergus back?"

"Yes. He's home." Jenny hugged herself. "He's – he's brought a friend with him."

Jenny turned her head and looked at her mother's neat profile. "A friend?"

"Yes. A girl called Rose. You may have seen her on television. She's an actress." A friend. A girl. An actress? "He met her a couple of months ago."

"H – have you met her?"

"No, but we've all been invited to a party there tomorrow night."

"But – but –" There didn't seem to be any words for the shock and the desolation which she felt. Mrs Fairburn stopped the car and turned to Jenny. "This is why I came to meet you at the station. I knew you'd be upset. I wanted to talk it over."

"I just – I just don't want him to bring anyone here to Creagan." Even to herself this sounded pathetically juvenile.

erbärmlich • kindisch

"Jenny, you don't own Fergus. He has a perfect right to make new friends. He's a grown man with his own life to live. Just as you have a life to make for yourself. You can't spend it looking over your shoulder and mourning for childhood fancies."

The worst bit was not that she actually said this, but that she had been so perceptive in the first place.

"I – I really do love him."

"I know. It's agony. First love is always agony. But you'll have to grit your teeth and see it through. And don't let anybody see how much you mind." They sat

deinen eigenen Weg finden musst • nachzutrauern • Kindheitsträumen • Es tut weh. • die Zähne zusammenbeißen • durchhalten

in silence for a bit. Then, "All right?" her mother asked, and Jenny nodded. Mrs Fairburn started the car up again, and they moved on.

"Do you think he'll marry her?"

"I've no idea. But from what Daphne Fenton tells me, it sounds perfectly possible. She says he's bought himself a flat in Wandsworth and Rose is making his loose covers."

Schonbezüge

"Do you think that's a bad sign?"

"Not bad, exactly. But indicative."

ein deutlicher Hinweis

Jenny fell silent. But as they turned into the gates of the Manse, she stirred herself. "Perhaps I shall like her."

"Yes," said Mrs Fairburn. "Perhaps you will."

Krankenhausserie • Langweilerin • Verzweiflung • Beben • distinguiert • ziemlich hübsch • sie hatte seidiges, schwarzes Haar

And she did try to like Rose. But it was difficult, because, without realising it, she had seen Rose on television in a hospital drama, where Rose had played a nurse. Even then Jenny had thought that she was a bore, with her heart-shaped face struggling with a variety of emotions, an unbearable distress being conveyed by a slight tremor in her well-bred voice.

In real life, Rose was pretty enough. Her hair was silky black, loose and curly around her shoulders, and she

**info**

Wenn to do vor ein Verb gestellt wird, wird dessen Bedeutung verstärkt. „Jenny did try to like Rose" heißt, dass Jenny sich wirklich bemühte, Rose zu mögen.

**Übung 52**

Bilden Sie die Verlaufsform der folgenden Verben. Aber aufgepasst, denn oft fällt das -e weg, wenn -ing angehängt wird!

| | |
|---|---|
| to marry | |
| to make | |
| to struggle | |
| to realise | |
| to change | |

wore a low-waisted dress with unexpected bits of beading and glitter stitched to its loose folds.

mit tief angesetzter Taille • vereinzelt • Perlen

"Fergus has told me so much about you," she said to Jenny when they were introduced at Inverbruie. "He says you were practically brought up together. Is your father a farmer too?"

"No, he's the bank manager in Creagan."

"And you've always lived here?"

"Born and bred. I even went to school here. I was in Edinburgh for the winter, but it's heaven to be back."

Ich bin hier geboren und aufgewachsen.

"Don't you get – er – rather bored in such a desolate spot?"

• äh

"No."

"What are you going to do now?"

"I don't know."

"Come to London. Nowhere else on earth to live, I always say to Fergy. Come to London and we'll keep an eye on you –" She reached out and closed her fingers around Fergus's arm. Fergus was at that moment engaged, happily, in conversation with somebody else, but she drew him physically away from this person and back to herself. "Darling, I was just saying, Jenny must come to London."

mitten in einem Gespräch • zog ihn regelrecht … weg

Fergus and Jenny looked into each other's eyes; Jenny smiled and found to her surprise that it was remarkably easy.

Fergus said, "Jenny doesn't like city life."

Jenny shrugged. "It's a matter of taste."

"But you can't stay here always." Rose sounded incredulous.

ungläubig

"I will for the summer." She had not, in fact, thought about it, but now discovered, in an instant, that her decision was made. "I'll get a holiday job in Creagan, I expect." She decided to change the subject. "My mother was telling me about the flat in Wandsworth."

"Yes …" Fergus began, but that was as far as he got because Rose took over.

"It's heavenly. Not very big, but full of sunshine. Just a few little touches and it will be quite perfect."

*Just a few little touches: nur noch der letzte Schliff*

"Has it got a garden?" Jenny asked.

"No. But there's a window box or two. I thought we could plant geraniums. Real scarlet ones. Then we can pretend we're in Majorca or Greece. Can't we, darling?"

*window box: Blumenkasten*

"Whatever you say," said Fergus.

Scarlet geraniums. 'Dear heaven,' thought Jenny, 'he really is in love with her.' And suddenly she couldn't bear to stand there any longer, watching them. She made her excuses and turned away. She did not speak to either Rose or Fergus for the rest of the evening.

But she could not escape Fergus, because he sought her out the very next day, spring-cleaning the summerhouse.

*sought her out: machte sie ... ausfindig • the very next day: gleich am nächsten Tag • spring-cleaning: beim Frühjahrsputz • rush mat: Binsenmatte • was startled into immobility: erstarrte sie zur Salzsäule*

"Jenny."

She was actually shaking dust out of a rush mat when he appeared, unexpectedly, around the side of the summerhouse, and for an instant she was startled into immobility.

"What do you want?" She managed at last.

"I've come to see you."

"How nice. Where's Rose?"

"She's at home. She's washing her hair."

"It looked perfectly clean to me."

"Jenny, are you going to listen to me?"

She sighed noisily and looked resigned. "It depends on what you've got to say."

"I just want you to understand. To understand the way things are. I want you not to be angry. I want to feel that we can still at least talk to each other. And be friends."

"Well, we're talking, aren't we?"

"And friends?"

"Oh, friends. Always friends. Friends whatever we do to each other."

"And what have I done?"
She glared at him accusingly, and then threw down the rush mat.
"All right, so you don't like Rose. You might as well admit it," he said.
"I don't feel about Rose one way or the other. I don't know Rose."
"Then isn't it a little unfair – on both Rose and myself – to make a snap judgment?"
"I just don't feel I have anything in common with her."
"That's just because she told you that you ought to get away from Creagan."
"And what possible business is it of hers?"
Now his temper was rising to match her own. She saw his jaw muscles tighten, a familiar sign, and she was pleased because she had made him angry. It somehow eased the hurt inside her.
"Jenny, you stay here for the rest of your life, and you'll end up a country bumpkin in a seated tweed skirt with nothing to talk about except dogs and fishing."
She turned on him. "You know something? I'd rather be that than a third-rate actress with a mouth like a button."

vorschnell zu urteilen

wurde seine Wut genauso groß wie ihre • linderte • Schmerz • Landpomeranze • ausgebeult • drittklassig • einem Knopfmund

**Übung 53**

Wie gut haben Sie aufgepasst? Sind die folgenden Aussagen wahr oder falsch? Tragen Sie ein T für true oder ein F für false in die Kästchen ein.

**1.** ☐ Daphne Fenton had invited the whole Fairburn family except Jenny to the party.
**2.** ☐ At the party Rose made it crystal clear that she and Fergus were a couple.
**3.** ☐ Fergus didn't want to lose Jenny as a friend.
**4.** ☐ Jenny's brother had always warned her not to waste her feelings on Fergus.
**5.** ☐ Both Jenny and Fergus were very emotional.

He laughed, but he was laughing at Jenny and not with her. He said unforgivably, "I do believe you're jealous. You always could be quite impossible!"

"And you, perhaps, could always be a fool, but I never realised it until now."

Fergus turned on his heel and walked away, across the lawn. Jenny watched his progress, her temper dying as swiftly as it had blown up. Words spoken in heat and haste were all very well, but they could never be taken back. Nothing could ever be the same again.

Jenny found a job in Creagan, working in a shop which sold Shetland pullovers and pebble-jewellery to tourists. Around July, she was told by her mother that Fergus and Rose were engaged, and were to be married in September in London where Rose's parents lived. Just a quiet wedding, with a few of their close London friends. But meantime, they had returned to Inverbruie and there was to be another little party and Jenny could not find the courage to go. After they were married, she told herself again, it would be different. She would become dynamic; go abroad perhaps; get a job in the French Alps as a chalet girl, or be a cook on a yacht. However, she was growing cold and there were trout to be caught for supper. She stood up, clambered down the heathery bank, untied the painter, pushed the boat out into the water and began to row.

Fishing was special, because when you fished you thought about nothing else. She took the boat a long way up the loch and then shipped the oars and let the wind drift her back towards the shore. Now, there was enough breeze to stir the surface of the water, and she began casting.

She heard the car coming up the road, but was too engrossed to pay attention to it. There was another bite or two, and then at last she hooked a fish, and concentrating on nothing else, began gently to reel it

etwas Unverzeihliches

drehte sich auf dem Absatz um • legte sich • in der Hitze des Gefechts • schön und gut

Bergkristallschmuck

inzwischen

aktiv werden • Zimmermädchen • Abendessen • kletterte ... herunter • Böschung • Fangleine • zog ... die Riemen ein • vertieft • es bissen noch einer oder zwei an • hatte sie einen Fisch am Haken • ihn ... einzuholen

in. She netted it out of the water, and dropped it in the bottom of the boat.
As if on cue, she heard a voice say, "Well done."
Startled by this interruption from the business in hand, she looked up and saw, all at once, a number of surprising things. She had, without realising it, drifted to within yards of the shore; the car she had heard on the road had stopped and was now parked a little way off; and Fergus, a solitary figure, stood on the bank and watched her.
He was bare-headed, the wind ruffling his dark hair. He wore a tweed jacket and a pair of corduroys, tucked into green rubber boots. Not dressed for fishing. Jenny sat in the rocking boat and looked at him, and wondered if he had come upon her by chance, or if, in fact, he had come looking, to ask why she had refused to come to the party, to try to persuade her to change her mind. If he did this, then they would have another argument, another row, and she knew that rather than repeat their last painful set-to, she would prefer never to have to speak to him again.
He grinned. He said again, "Well done. You handled that very neatly. I couldn't have done better myself."
Jenny did not reply. Instead, she busied herself in reeling

fischte ihn aus dem Wasser • wie aufs Stichwort • zu erledigend • bis auf mehrere Yard (1 Yard = 0,91 Meter) • etwas entfernt • einsam • barhäuptig • zerzauste

Streit • Krach

Das hast du super hingekriegt.

**Übung 54**

Jenny und Fergus scheinen Meister im Streiten zu sein. Welche Substantive drücken das Thema Streit aus? Umkreisen Sie die richtigen Wörter aus der unten angegebenen Auswahl.

| | |
|---|---|
| quarrel | interruption |
| dispute | row |
| set-to | change of mind |
| argument | temper |

in the loose line, securing the barbed fly. With care, she laid down the rod, and then looked up again at Fergus.

*mit Widerhaken versehen*

She said, "How long have you been there?"

"Ten minutes or more." He put his hands in his jacket pockets. "I came to find you. Your mother told me you'd come up here. I want to talk to you."

"What about?"

"Jenny, don't get your hackles up. Let's call it pax."

*stell … deine Stacheln auf • Frieden schließen*

It seemed only fair. "All right."

"Come and get me then."

Jenny made no move to do this, but even as they spoke she was being blown inshore, and as she hesitated, she felt the first bump as the keel touched stone. Before she realised what was happening, Fergus had waded out and grabbed the bow, thrown one long leg over the gunwale and was aboard.

*Kiel • auf Grund lief • Bug • Dollbord*

"Now," he said, "give me the oars."

There didn't seem to be very much alternative. With a couple of clean strokes, he had turned the light craft, and then they were headed back out into the middle of the loch. It was ten minutes or so before he looked

*Schlägen • Boot*

**Übung 55** Setzen Sie die wörtliche Rede in die indirekte Rede. Achten Sie auf die Anpassung der Zeitformen und der Pronomen.

1. "How long have you been here?"
   Jenny asked Fergus ______________________.
2. "I came to find you. Your mother told me you'd come up here." Fergus told Jenny ______________________
   ______________________.
3. "Jenny, don't get your hackles up. Let's call it pax."
   Fergus told Jenny ______________________
   ______________________.

about him, decided they had come far enough, shipped the oars, and turned up the collar of his jacket against the cold edge of the wind.

"Now," he said, "we're going to talk."

It seemed sensible to take the initiative. "I suppose my mother told you that I didn't want to come tonight. I suppose that's what it's all about."

sensible – vernünftig

"Yes, it's about that. And other things, too."

She waited for him to enlarge on this, but he did not continue. Across the thwarts, they looked at each other, and then suddenly smiled. And all at once Jenny was filled with a curious contentment and peace. It was a long time since she'd sat in a boat with Fergus, in the middle of the loch, with the familiar hills folding away on all sides and the sky arched above them, and have him smile at her like that. It made it easier to be honest, not only with him, but with herself.

thwarts – Ruderbank

"It's just that I don't want to come. I don't want to see Rose again. It'll be different when you're married to her. But now …" She shrugged. "It's cowardice, I suppose," she finally admitted.

cowardice – Feigheit

"That doesn't sound like you."

"Perhaps it isn't me. Perhaps I'm all twisted and back to front. You said that day by the summerhouse that I was jealous, and, of course, you were quite right. I suppose I always thought of you as my property, but that's wrong, isn't it? No person can ever belong to another person, even after they're married."

twisted – verdreht • back to front – durcheinander

"No man is an island."

No man is an island. – Niemand ist eine Insel.

"I always thought that bits of a man had to be an island. You can't creep inside somebody else's head."

"No. You can't do that."

"Just like you can't go on being a child. You have to grow up whether you want to or not."

He said, "Did you get that job in Creagan?"

"Yes, but it folds up in October when the shop closes down for the winter. I've decided that then I shall be

it folds up – ist es vorbei

enormously enterprising and find myself an occupation that's very well paid and miles away. Like America or Switzerland." She smiled, wryly. "Rose would approve of that."

Fergus stayed silent. His eyes, watching her, were unblinking, intensely blue.

"And how," she asked politely, "is Rose?"

"I don't know."

Jenny frowned. "But you have to know. She's at Inverbruie."

"She's not at Inverbruie."

"She's not …?" A curlew flew overhead, its cry mournful, and the water slapped and whispered against the planking of the boat. "But Mother said …"

"She got it wrong. My mother didn't say anything about Rose being here; your mother just took it for granted that Rose was with me. We're not going to get married. The engagement's off."

"Off? You mean –? But why didn't Mother tell me?"

"She didn't know. I haven't got around to telling my own parents yet. I wanted to tell you before I told anyone else."

For some reason, this was so touching that Jenny

unternehmungslustig • ironisch

flog über sie hinweg • plätscherte • Bootsplanken • hielt es für selbstverständlich • ist geplatzt • dazu gekommen

bewegend

**Übung 56** Wie können die folgenden Wendungen anders ausgedrückt werden? Kreuzen Sie die richtige Erklärung an.

**1.** Rose would approve of Jenny finding herself an occupation that was well paid and far away.
- [ ] Rose would give her permission for Jenny to do that.
- [ ] Rose would favour such a decision.

**2.** Jenny's mother got it wrong.
- [ ] Jenny's mother had misunderstood something.
- [ ] Mrs Fairburn had told her daughter a lie.

wondered if she were about to burst into tears. "But, why? Why, Fergus?"
"You just said it. No person can belong to another person."
"Didn't – didn't you love her?"
"Yes, I did. I loved her very much." He could say that, and she didn't feel jealous in the least, just sad for him because it hadn't worked out. "But you marry a life as well as a person, and Rose's life and mine seemed to run along parallel lines, like railway tracks, without ever actually touching."
"When did all this happen?"
"A couple of weeks ago. That's why I came north for the weekend; I wanted to explain it to my parents, and let my mother see I wasn't dying of a broken heart."
"And aren't you?"
"Perhaps a little bit, but not enough to show."
"Rose loved you."
"For a bit she did, yes."
Jenny hesitated, and then said it. "*I* love you."

kein bisschen • geklappt

Eisenbahnschienen

It was Fergus's turn to look as though he were about to burst into tears. "Oh, Jenny."
"You might as well know. You've probably always known. I never thought I could say that to anybody, least of all to you, but for some reason it seems to be quite easy. I mean, you don't have to do anything about it, but you might as well know. It doesn't change anything. I shall still find that marvellous job and winkle myself away from Creagan into the wide, wide world."
She smiled, expecting him to smile back at her, approving of this sensible, mature scheme. But he did not smile. For a long moment he simply looked at her, and she felt her own smile die beneath the sadness in his face. Then he said, "Don't."
Jenny frowned. "But, Fergus, I thought that was what

jetzt war Fergus dran zu

mich ... loseisen

you wanted. For me to get away from Creagan, and stand on my own feet."

"I couldn't bear you to go away and stand on your own feet," he told her bluntly.

"Well, whose feet am I going to stand on?"

The absurdity of her question somehow made everything all right again. He was caught unawares by this absurdity, and despite himself, began to laugh, wryly, as much at himself as at her. "I don't know. I suppose mine. The truth is, that you've been part of my life for so long that I don't think I can bear the thought of your going away and leaving us all. Leaving me. Life would be so dreadfully dull. There'd be nobody to argue with. Nobody to yell at. Nobody to make me laugh."

überrumpelt worden • gegen seinen Willen

Jenny thought about this. She said, "You know, if I had an ounce of pride, I would go away. I'd be the sort of girl who didn't want to be loved on the rebound from some other person."

Fünkchen • von jemandem geliebt werden ..., der noch nicht über jemand anderen hinweg ist

"If you had an ounce of pride, you wouldn't have told me that you loved me."

"You must have known."

"I only know that you were there long before Rose."

"So what was Rose?"

Fergus fell silent. Then he said tentatively, "A pause in the conversation?"

zögernd

"Oh, Fergus."

"I – I think I'm asking you to marry me. We've wasted enough time as it is. Perhaps I should have had the sense to do it a long time ago."

so klug sein sollen • weise

"No." She was suddenly very wise. "A long time ago would have been too soon. I thought you belonged to me then. But now, like I said, I know that nobody can ever belong to anybody else. Not totally. And yet, it's only when you think that you're going to lose something that you realise how precious it is."

"I found that out too," said Fergus. "What a very good thing that we both found it out at the same time."

Out in the middle of the water, it was becoming chilly. Jenny, despite herself, shivered.
"You're cold," said Fergus. "I'll take you back." He reached for the oars, took his bearings with a glance over his shoulder and turned the little boat.
Jenny suddenly remembered. "But I can't go back yet, Fergus. I've only caught one trout and we'll need three for supper."
"To hell with supper. We'll go out. We'll take all the parents and I'll stand the lot of you dinner at the Creagan Arms. We might even rustle up some champagne and it can be an engagement party – if you like!"
Now they were heading home, back towards the mooring, the little craft skimming across the choppy waters of the loch. The wind blew from behind her. She turned up the collar of her jacket and dug her hands deep into its capacious pockets. She smiled at her love. She said, "I like."

took his bearings: orientierte sich
stand the lot of you dinner: lade euch alle zum Abendessen ein • rustle up: auftreiben
mooring: Anlegeplatz • skimming across: schoss über • choppy: bewegt

**Übung 57**

Zum Schluss wendet sich doch noch alles zum Guten für Jenny und Fergus. Testen Sie noch einmal Ihr Englisch und korrigieren Sie die fünf grammatischen Fehler, die sich im Text versteckt haben.

Jennys dream did come true in the end. She had known Fergus for so long that it didn't mattered that he had only recent split up from Rose. Fergus had realised that he had wasted a lot of time and didn't want Jenny to leave from Creagan. They would surprise their family's with the news of their engagement.

# Lösungen

**1**

| | | | | | | | | | | | | | | |
|---|---|---|---|---|---|---|---|---|---|---|---|---|---|---|
| | | | | | | 1 | | | | | | | | |
| 4 | D | I | L | E | M | M | A | | | | | | | |
| | | | | | | O | | | | | | | | |
| | | | | | | T | | | | | | | | |
| | | | | | | O | | | | | | 3 | | |
| | | | | 5 | C | R | A | V | E | | | P | | |
| | | | | | | W | | | | 2 | | L | | |
| | | | | | 6 | A | W | E | S | T | R | U | C | K |
| | | | | | | Y | | | | E | | C | | |
| | | | | | | | | | | A | | K | | |
| | | | | | | | | | | S | | Y | | |
| | | | | | | | | | | E | | | | |

**2**

1. [X] **disapproval of** — [ ] approval of — [ ] dislike of
2. [X] **intended to** — [ ] wanted to — [ ] remembered to
3. [ ] very upset — [ ] very sad — [X] **very anxious**

**3**

1. [F] Tom felt like returning to London as he didn't want to go north without Elaine. (Tom wäre am liebsten nach London zurückgekehrt, weil er nicht ohne Elaine gen Norden fahren wollte.)
2. [T] **The time without Elaine would help Tom to get a different perspective on their relationship.**
   (Die Zeit ohne Elaine würde Tom helfen, ihre Beziehung aus einer anderen Perspektive zu sehen.)
3. [F] Tom's cousin Kitty had been a rebel in her youth but in the end she became a chartered accountant.
   (Toms Kusine Kitty war in ihrer Jugend eine Rebellin gewesen, aber letztendlich wurde sie Wirtschaftsprüferin.)
4. [T] **Tom had been surprised to hear that Kitty of all people had got married.**
   (Tom war überrascht gewesen, als er hörte, dass gerade Kitty geheiratet hatte.)
5. [T] **Aunt Mabel had always been so kind to him that there was no way he wouldn't travel up to her birthday party.**
   (Tante Mabel war immer so nett zu ihm gewesen, dass es absolut nicht drin war, nicht zu ihrer Geburtstagsparty zu fahren.)
6. [F] Tom and Kitty were only a year apart in age.
   (Tom und Kitty lagen altersmäßig nur ein Jahr auseinander.)
7. [T] **Kitty had always listened to what Tom had said.**
   (Kitty hatte immer auf Tom gehört.)

8. [F] Tom was convinced that Elaine and Kitty would get along being so alike.
(Tom war davon überzeugt, dass sich Elaine und Kitty verstehen würden, da sie sich so ähnlich waren.)
9. [F] Tom had some sad memories of his childhood days in Northumberland.
(Tom hatte einige traurige Erinnerungen an seine Kindheitstage in Northumberland.)

**4**

1. Fortunately the children were not supervised by the adults, they could play **unchecked**.
2. The children pretended that the oil was real but it was just **make-believe**.
3. They slept in a tent that was not the real thing, it was only **make-shift**.
4. Aunt Mabel had not been **blessed** with children of her own.

**5**

1. curtains – carpets – ~~**geraniums**~~ – wallpapers
   Alle anderen Wörter beschreiben etwas, das in Mabels Burg erneuert wurde.
2. renew – change – transform – ~~**display**~~
   Alle anderen Verben beschreiben eine Art des Renovierens.
3. ~~**subsequently**~~ – interior – structural – new
   Alle anderen Wörter sind Adjektive.

**6**

| | | | |
|---|---|---|---|
| 1. experience | [X] **Erfahrung** | [ ] Experiment | [X] **Erlebnis** |
| 2. construct | [ ] bilden | [X] **bauen** | [X] **zusammenstellen** |
| 3. landing | [X] **Landung** | [ ] Ausladen | [X] **Treppenabsatz** |
| 4. elaborate | [X] **näher eingehen auf**<br>[X] **ausarbeiten** | | [X] **kunstvoll** |

**7**

to rub **together**
to do **up**
to slap **on**
to break **up**
to stay **with**

**8**

1. Mabel was told that the man with the glasses had arrived. Who was he?
   [X] **It was a man who brought glasses for the party.**
   **Es war ein Mann, der Gläser für die Party brachte.**
   [ ] It was a man who was wearing glasses but was otherwise unknown.
   Dies ist die falsche Antwort, aber da **glasses** auch **Brille** bedeutet, kann durchaus Verwirrung entstehen!

2. What kind of room was the nursery at Kinton?
   [ ] A place where plants and trees were grown.
   Eine **nursery** kann in einem anderen Zusammenhang auch **Gärtnerei** bedeuten.
   [X] **A room where the children played.**
   In diesem Fall handelt es sich um ein **Kinderzimmer**.

**9**
1. For practical reasons Kitty had tied back her hair into a **ponytail**.
2. The branch of spruce wasn't as flexible as Kitty wanted it to be, it was quite **recalcitrant**.
3. Kitty was concentrating so hard, she actually looked as if she was in pain or **agonised**.
4. The **ceiling** was draped with garden netting.

**10**
1. Kitty was very **cautious** in disentangling herself from the ivy.
2. Kitty had worked very **hard**.
   (Aufgepasst, **hard** heißt **schwer**, aber **hardly** heißt **kaum**!)
3. She knew it had been really **stupid** of her to get married to Terence.
4. **Stupidly** she had married Terence.

**11** The kitchen was buzzing with activity. Several **men** and women were preparing food for Aunt Mabel's **seventieth** birthday party. Some **were beating** egg whites for a cake. Kitty's **teenage** son Crispin was busy eating leftovers. He told Tom that he and his mother lived in a caravan but **that they were going to move in with Aunt Mabel after the party**.

**12**
1. Tom was **lying** on his bed.
   (Tom lag auf seinem Bett.)
2. He had **laid** the pyjamas on top of his bed.
   (Er hatte die Pyjamas auf sein Bett gelegt.)
3. He liked to **lie** there and listen to the rain.
   (Er lag gerne da und hörte dem Regen zu.)

**13**

| noun | verb | adjective |
|---|---|---|
| **exhaustion** | to exhaust | exhausting |
| continuation | to continue | **continuing** |
| drive | to drive | **driving** |
| progress | **to progress** | progressive |
| **imagination** | to imagine | imaginative |
| thought | to think | **thoughtful** |

**14** Tom thought it looked very

1. C **OTTAGE**
2. **SC** H **OOLMASTER**
3. **SL** A **VE**
4. **HAWTH** O **RN**
5. T **ANG**
6. **VARN** I **SH**
7. C **HEERFUL**

**15**
1. to build – **to pull down**
2. ugly – **handsome**
3. spacious – **cramped**
4. to get undressed – **to get dressed**
5. to throw away – **to save**
6. unpleasant – **nice**

**16**
1. Why is Tom worried about Kitty?
   (Warum macht sich Tom solche Sorgen um Kitty?)
   [F] He thinks Kitty is physically too weak to do the work.
   (Er meint, Kitty ist körperlich zu schwach für die Arbeit.)
   [T] **He feels she has taken on too much.**
   (Er meint, dass sie sich zu viel aufgehalst hat.)

2. Why does Kitty have to dig the garden?
   (Warum muss Kitty den Garten umgraben?)
   [T] **She has to unearth all the things that are buried.**
   (Sie muss all die vergrabenen Dinge ausgraben.)
   [F] The cultivator has broken down after the first try.
   (Der Kultivator hat beim ersten Versuch schlappgemacht.)

3. Why is Kitty so short of money?
   (Warum ist Kitty so knapp bei Kasse?)
   [F] Two of the reasons are Crispin's school fees and paying off debts.
   (Zwei der Gründe sind Crispins Schulgebühren und das Abzahlen der Schulden.)
   [T] **After the divorce she was left with little money.**
   (Nach der Scheidung blieb ihr nicht viel Geld.)

4. Why is Kitty estranged from her parents?
   (Warum ist Kitty ihren Eltern entfremdet?)
   [T] **She is very different from what they would have liked her to be and they never truly accepted her.**
   (Sie ist ganz anders, als sie sie gerne gehabt hätten, und sie haben sie nie wirklich akzeptiert.)
   [F] They have distanced themselves after her divorce.
   (Sie haben sich nach ihrer Scheidung distanziert.)

**17**
1. Kitty didn't want Tom to **remind** her of the evening when he had invited her and Terence for dinner.
2. Tom didn't **remember** Kitty ever having been so upset.
3. They both **remembered** the happy days of their childhood.

**18**

1. d As a teenager **Kitty had been one of the wildest of the children.**
   Als Teenager war Kitty eines der wildesten Kinder gewesen.
2. e He couldn't bare seeing her so upset. **He took her in his arms and comforted her.**
   Er konnte es nicht ertragen, sie so niedergeschlagen zu sehen. Er nahm sie ihn seine Arme und tröstete sie.
3. c Kitty needed various things for her house. **Tom wanted to take her to an antique shop and buy her something.**
   Kitty brauchte verschiedene Dinge für ihr Haus. Tom wollte mit ihr in einen Antiquitätenladen gehen und ihr etwas kaufen.
4. f There where times **when Kitty was close to giving up.**
   Es gab Zeiten, da war Kitty kurz vor dem Aufgeben.
5. a Aunt Mabel had always thought they would make a nice couple. **Kitty was too young and too bouncy for Tom at the time.**
   Tante Mabel hatte immer schon gefunden, dass sie ein schönes Paar abgeben würden. Kitty war damals zu jung und zu lebhaft für Tom.
6. b Kitty, Tom and the other nephews and nieces **had made up for the fact that Mabel and Ned had no children of their own.**
   Kitty, Tom und die anderen Neffen und Nichten hatten es ausgeglichen, dass Mabel und Ned keine eigenen Kinder hatten.

**19**

1. The castle was always full of other **people's** children.
   **Other peoples' children** bedeutet **die Kinder anderer Völker**!
2. Mabel had **held** it all together for a long time.
   **Hold** ist ein unregelmäßiges Verb, mit der Form **held** im Past Tense und im Past Participle.
3. She had stuck to what she believed **in**.
   **An etwas glauben** heißt **to believe in something**.
4. Kitty and Mabel were very similar in **many** ways.
   Aufgepasst, **much** wird nur bei unzählbaren Substantiven verwendet.
5. Deep in thought Tom drove back **slowly** to Kinton.
   Hier muss ein Adverb stehen, kein Adjektiv.

**20**

1. Without her glasses Mabel could hardly see the print, she was **p** e e **r** i **n g** at it.
2. Mabel wouldn't have to walk far to do part of her shopping as she was going to live so close to the **b** u **t c h** e **r**.
3. The whole castle was in a bad state, from the tower to the **b** a **s** e **m** e **n t**.

**21**

| **adjective** | **adverb** |
|---|---|
| marvellous | **marvellously** |
| keen | **keenly** |
| complicated | **in a complicated way** |
| slow | **slowly** |
| late | **late**<br>(„Lately" heißt „in letzter Zeit"!) |

**22**

| | | | | | | | | | | | |
|---|---|---|---|---|---|---|---|---|---|---|---|
| i | w | n | b | t | i | b | t | x | z | q | o |
| e | i | r | u | s | t | l | e | q | w | z | v |
| r | v | n | i | s | i | k | s | p | o | t | t |
| g | d | n | u | s | y | e | r | v | b | e | s |
| v | i | e | j | m | t | m | w | e | d | l | e |
| p | s | c | r | k | i | m | p | v | w | z | i |
| n | a | k | g | i | n | f | i | r | m | t | l |
| o | p | l | s | l | y | f | w | y | i | a | i |
| u | p | i | f | v | e | z | j | u | i | n | p |
| p | e | n | h | k | e | y | j | i | t | e | t |
| k | a | e | i | w | e | n | i | l | l | p | r |
| y | r | f | h | p | n | c | y | l | w | m | l |

**23**

**1.** curve – arch – ~~sound~~ – hall
Alle anderen Wörter beschreiben das Innere von Kinton.

**2.** to descend – to go down – ~~to smooth down~~ – to start down
Alle anderen Verben bedeuten „hinuntergehen".

**3.** candle – ~~champagne~~ – fire – flame
Alle anderen Wörter sind eine Lichtquelle.

**4.** ~~splendour~~ – joy – pleasure – satisfaction
Alle anderen Substantive sind ein Ausdruck von Toms Gefühlen.

**5.** blue – ~~funny~~ – enormous – unblinking
Alle anderen Adjektive beschreiben Kittys Augen.

**24**

**1.** Why is Kitty floundering?
(Warum stammelt Kitty?)
[F] She is not sure of her feelings for Tom.
(Sie ist sich ihrer Gefühle für Tom nicht sicher.)
[F] She knows Tom is still in another relationship.
(Sie weiß, dass Tom noch in einer anderen Beziehung steckt.)
[T] **She is afraid he feels pity for her and might change his mind.**
(Sie befürchtet, dass er sie bemitleidet und seine Meinung ändern könnte.)

**2.** Why is Mabel going to leave Kinton?
(Warum wird Mabel Kinton verlassen?)
[F] She has decided to retire in France.
(Sie hat beschlossen, ihren Ruhestand in Frankreich zu verbringen.)
[T] **The castle is too big for her and in need of a lot of repair.**
(Das Schloss ist zu groß für sie, und es stehen viele Reparaturen an.)
[F] Someone has made her a good offer for it.
(Jemand hat ihr ein gutes Angebot dafür gemacht.)

**3.** Why is Tom ready to change his life for Kitty?
(Warum ist Tom dazu bereit, sein Leben für Kitty zu verändern?)
[F] She reminds him of his happy childhood.
(Sie erinnert ihn an seine glückliche Kindheit.)

[T] **He realises that he feels happy, full of joy and satisfied in Kitty's presence.**
(Ihm wird bewusst, dass er in Kittys Gegenwart glücklich, voller Freude und zufrieden ist.)
[F] Aunt Mabel has convinced him that she is the right partner for him.
(Tante Mabel hat ihn davon überzeugt, dass sie die richtige Partnerin für ihn ist.)

**25**
trout – **trouts oder trout**
godchild – **godchildren**
church – **churches**
picnic – **picnics**
tea-party – **tea-parties**
bus – **buses**
person – **people** oder **persons**
country – **countries**
life – **lives**
heather – **Hier gibt es natürlich keine Pluralform, da Heide im Englischen wie im Deutschen unzählbar ist.**

**26**
1. oh my goodness – **my** (= ach du meine Güte)
2. a covering for the head that is knitted out of wool – **woollen hat** (= Wollmütze)
3. great pleasure or enjoyment – **delight** (= Freude)
4. to change and become something different – **to turn into** (= werden)

**27**
Mrs Farquhar is **Rory's grandmother.**
Rory is **Mrs Farquhar's grandson.**
Mary Reekie is **Mrs Farquhar's cook.**
Effie McLaren is **the owner of the village shop.**
Roger is **one of Lavinia's brothers.**

**28**
1. Lavinia thought the nurse might **send her packing**.
(Lavinia dachte, die Krankenschwester würde sie vielleicht rausschmeißen.)
☐ The nurse might tell her to pack her things.
☒ **The nurse might tell her to go.**
☐ The nurse might be rude to her.

2. Stella Felham … I **would** meet her.
(Ausgerechnet ihr musste ich begegnen.)
☒ **Of all people I had to meet her.**
☐ I expected to meet her.
☐ I thought I would meet her.

**29**
1. Stella Felham told Lavinia to come and visit as her husband had nothing to do and was **bored stiff**.
2. He would like to have a **glimpse** of Lavinia.
3. Lionel's fishing trip didn't take place as planned. It was **called off**.
4. Mrs Felham was shocked to hear that Lavinia was going to visit Mrs Farquhar. Her voice **rose an octave**.

**30** 1. conservatory
2. half landing
3. passage
4. sweater
5. disinfectant

**31** 1. F Lavinia is disappointed to get such a frosty reception from Rory.
(Lavinia ist enttäuscht, von Rory so frostig empfangen zu werden.)
2. T **Rory and Lavinia catch up on what has been happening in their lives.**
(Rory und Lavinia erzählen sich, was inzwischen in ihrem Leben passiert ist.)
3. F Mrs Felham was the one who informed Rory that his grandmother was ill.
(Mrs Felham war diejenige, die Rory informiert hat, dass seine Großmutter krank war.)
4. F Rory was in New York when the letter with the bad news arrived.
(Rory war in New York, als der Brief mit den schlechten Nachrichten eintraf.)
5. T **Lavinia's parents used to rent a cottage from Rory's grandmother.**
(Lavinias Eltern mieteten früher ein Häuschen von Rorys Großmutter.)
6. F Apart from her present job as a private nurse Lavinia works in a hospital.
(Abgesehen von ihrer momentanen Stelle als Privatpflegerin arbeitet Lavinia in einem Krankenhaus.)
7. T **The sound of Rory's name evokes fond memories for Lavinia and makes her heart pound.**
(Rorys Name weckt schöne Erinnerungen in Lavinia und bringt ihr Herz zum Hämmern.)

**32** 1. The nurse asked Rory: "Could you please **lend** me your car?"
2. Rory said: "No problem, you can **borrow** it anytime."
3. Rory had no problem **lending** his car.

**33** 1. stale – warm – ~~pale~~ – muggy
(Alle anderen Adjektive beschreiben das Wetter.)
2. platform – passenger – luggage – ~~newsstand~~
(Alles andere hat mit der Zugreise zu tun.)
3. tweed coat – ~~leaves~~ – brooch – felt hat
(Alles andere hat die Dame an, die mit Claudia im Abteil sitzt.)
4. to wear – ~~to walk~~ – to leave – to make
(Alles andere sind unregelmäßige Verben.)

**34**

| Present Tense | Past Tense | Past Participle |
|---|---|---|
| to bring | brought | **brought** |
| to know | **knew** | known |
| to lay | **laid** | laid |
| to blow | blew | **blown** |

**35**

1. in a vulgar way – **genteelly**
2. to get off – **to climb aboard**
3. to get on – **to alight**
4. to unpack – **to pack up**
5. close – **distant**
6. to set – **to rise**
7. tiny – **capacious**

**36**

1 Claudia shared the second part of her journey with a lady who kept her entertained.
2 She told her that she had visited her sister and done some shopping.
3 In the course of their conversation they established that the lady knew Jennifer.
4 She approved of Jennifer's husband Ronnie even though he wasn't Scottish.
5 At their destination the lady was picked up by her husband, the shepherd, but there was no sign of Jennifer.
6 Claudia was slightly disappointed.
7 However she was pretty surprised when she saw who was waiting for her.
8 Magnus had changed but she still recognised him, even after all these years.
9 Magnus told Claudia that Jennifer hadn't been able to collect her because of a problem with the boiler.

**37**

| | | | |
|---|---|---|---|
| 1. statement | [X] **Aussage** | [ ] Staat | [X] **Bankauszug** |
| 2. close | [X] **nah** | [X] **schwül** | [X] **eng** |
| 3. air | [X] **Luft** | [X] **Ausstrahlung** | [X] **Melodie** |
| 4. to run | [X] **rinnen** | [X] **rennen** | [X] **leiten** |

**38**

| | | | | | | | | | | |
|---|---|---|---|---|---|---|---|---|---|---|
| | | | | 2 | | | | | | |
| | | | | H | | | | | | |
| | | 3 | C | A | L | M | L | Y | | |
| | | | 1 | R | | | | | | |
| 4 | T | R | A | D | E | | | | | |
| | | | S | | | | | | | |
| | | | H | | | | | | | |
| | | | A | | | | | | | |
| 5 | C | O | M | M | I | S | S | I | O | N |
| | | | E | | | | | | | |
| | | | D | | | | | | | |

**39**

1. a twelve month's supply of jellies and jams
   [ ] jellies and jams to sell for a year
   [X] **enough jellies and jams to last a year**

2. I have to sort out a few things.
   [X] **I have to take care of a few things.**
   [ ] I have to get rid of a few things.

**40** It was hard to believe but Claudia had never met Jennifer's children, **Ronnie**, Jane, Rory and Geordie, before. Jennifer was thrilled Claudia would finally get to know them. She was also excited and keen to show Claudia all the new things in the **flat**, among them the bedspreads that she had discovered in a **wooden chest** in the attic. She was a little **envious though that Claudia was so independent and successful and had such stylish clothes**. She also **admired Claudia for being so slim**. However she was aware of Claudia's unsteady relationship with Giles whom she had met once when she was visiting her in London. **They had never been very open with each other** so she **carefully** quizzed Claudia about her surprise visit. She **realised though that she might not tell her what was really going on**.

**41** to slam **shut**
to see to **lunch**
to cut **loose**
to gather **up**
to call **out**

**42** filthy – **clean**
narrow – **wide**
stolid – **energetic**
perhaps – **definitely**
rounded – **pointed**

**43**
1. razorbill – ~~seaweed~~ – ladybird – sea urchin
   Alles andere sind Tiere.
2. mud – laughter – ~~window~~ – moss
   Die anderen Substantive sind nicht zählbar.
3. Rory – Jennifer – ~~Magnus~~ – Claudia
   Alle anderen sind miteinander verwandt.
4. ~~to kiss~~ – to feed – to eat – to smell
   Alle anderen sind unregelmäßige Verben.

**44**
1. [d] It was such a beautiful day. **Claudia couldn't bear to waste a moment of it.**
2. [e] The dog was happy. **Finally someone paid attention to it.**
3. [a] Magnus suggested climbing the hill. **That was exactly what Claudia had wanted to do.**
4. [b] The children went home with their mother. **They wanted to watch a TV programme.**
5. [c] The turf was firm. **It was pleasant to walk on it.**

**45**

| noun | verb | adjective |
|---|---|---|
| length | **to lengthen** | long |
| frost | to frost | **frosty** |
| shade | to shade | **shady** |
| chill | **to chill** | chilly |
| breath | **to breathe** | breathtaking |

**46**

1. Magnus used to tell his **mates** that Claudia was his first love.
2. When they were young they had all their lives in front of them – the world was their **oyster**.
3. Just like Magnus, Claudia thought she was too old for **pride**.
4. Claudia didn't want to cause Magnus any **pain** by telling him about Giles.
5. Magnus looked as if he needed someone to **comfort** him.
6. Claudia didn't want to **unload** her problems on to Magnus after he had confessed that she was his only love.
7. Her **state of mind** was one of confusion and distress.

**47**

1. [F] Claudia fainted when she read the headlines in the Social Diary of the paper.
   (Claudia wurde ohnmächtig, als sie die Schlagzeilen auf der Gesellschaftsseite der Zeitung las.)
2. [T] **Giles had not even had the decency to let Claudia know that he was getting married.**
   (Giles hatte noch nicht einmal den Anstand gehabt, Claudia wissen zu lassen, dass er heiraten würde.)
3. [F] Giles had known his bride for more than a year.
   (Giles kannte seine Braut seit mehr als einem Jahr.)
4. [T] **Magnus didn't realise what he would trigger by buying the paper.**
   (Magnus ahnte nicht, was er auslösen würde, als er die Zeitung kaufte.)
5. [T] **Claudia had fooled herself into believing that she had a future with Giles.**
   (Claudia hatte sich etwas vorgemacht, indem sie glaubte, dass sie und Giles eine Zukunft hätten.)

**48**

| | | | | | | | | | | | |
|---|---|---|---|---|---|---|---|---|---|---|---|
| l | p | t | **b** | **e** | **r** | **r** | **y** | x | z | q | **r** |
| n | o | b | u | s | t | l | e | q | w | z | **e** |
| r | **v** | **o** | **i** | **c** | **e** | k | s | t | o | t | **l** |
| g | d | n | **n** | s | y | e | r | v | b | l | **i** |
| v | i | e | **u** | m | t | v | **w** | e | d | l | **e** |
| **e** | s | c | **m** | k | i | t | p | **h** | w | z | **f** |
| **x** | a | k | **b** | i | n | **s** | i | r | **e** | t | l |
| **c** | k | l | s | l | y | f | **w** | y | i | **e** | i |
| **u** | l | i | f | v | e | z | j | **e** | i | n | **l** |
| **s** | **c** | **r** | **e** | **a** | **m** | s | j | x | **e** | g | t |
| **e** | b | e | i | w | e | n | i | m | l | **t** | r |
| x | y | f | h | p | v | c | o | l | w | l | **s** |

**49**

| | | | |
|---|---|---|---|
| **1.** kind | [X] **Sorte** | [ ] Kind | [X] **nett** |
| **2.** receiver | [X] **Telefonhörer** | [X] **Empfänger** | [ ] Empfang |
| **3.** bright | [X] **fröhlich** | [X] **hell** | [X] **klug** |
| **4.** battered | [X] **verbeult** | [X] **missbraucht** | [X] **in Teig gewälzt** |
| **5.** to collect | [X] **sammeln** | [X] **abholen** | [ ] zusammenstellen |

**50**

**1.** Jenny had known Fergus for ages, they used to both laugh and **quarrel**.
**2.** Fergus was the one who **persuaded** her parents to allow Jenny to leave boarding school and come home.
**3.** Jenny had lots of **schemes** for Fergus' and her future life together.
**4.** But Fergus went to Edinburgh and **qualified** as a chartered accountant.

**51**

strange – **odd**
maybe – **perhaps**
too – **as well**
realise – **recognise**
lean out – **hang out**
normally – **usually**

**52**

| | |
|---|---|
| to marry | marrying |
| to make | making |
| to struggle | struggling |
| to realise | realising |
| to change | changing |

**53**

**1.** [F] Daphne Fenton had invited the whole Fairburn family except Jenny to the party.
(Daphne Fenton hatte die ganze Familie Fairburn außer Jenny zu der Party eingeladen.)

**2.** [T] **At the party Rose made it crystal clear that she and Fergus were a couple.**
(Bei der Party machte es Rose völlig klar, dass sie und Fergus ein Paar waren.)

**3.** [T] **Fergus didn't want to lose Jenny as a friend.**
(Fergus wollte Jenny nicht als Freundin verlieren.)

**4.** [F] Jenny's brother had always warned her not to waste her feelings on Fergus.
(Jennys Bruder hatte sie immer davor gewarnt, ihre Gefühle an Fergus zu verschwenden.)
Jenny ist Einzelkind!

**5.** [T] **Both Jenny and Fergus were very emotional.**
(Sowohl Jenny als auch Fergus waren sehr emotional.)

**54**

| | |
|---|---|
| **quarrel** | interruption |
| **dispute** | row |
| **set-to** | change of mind |
| **argument** | temper |

**55**
**1.** "How long have you been here?"
Jenny asked Fergus **how long he had been here**.
**2.** I came to find you. Your mother told me you'd come up here."
Fergus told Jenny **that he had come to find her and that her mother had told him that she had come up here.**
**3.** "Jenny, don't get your hackles up. Let's call it pax."
Fergus told Jenny **that she shouldn't get her hackles up. He suggested they call it pax.**

**56**
**1.** Rose would **approve of** Jenny finding herself an occupation that was well paid and far away.
☐ Rose would give her permission for Jenny to do that.
☒ **Rose would favour such a decision**

**2.** Jenny's mother **got it wrong**.
☒ **Jenny's mother had misunderstood something.**
☐ Mrs Fairburn had told her daughter a lie.

**57** ~~Jennys~~ **Jenny's** dream did come true in the end. She had known Fergus for so long that it didn't ~~mattered~~ **matter** that he had only ~~recent~~ **recently** split up from Rose. Fergus had realised that he had wasted a lot of time and didn't want Jenny to leave ~~from~~ Creagan. They would surprise their ~~family's~~ **families** with the news of their engagement.

# Wörterverzeichnis

## A

to achieve something etwas schaffen
aching schmerzend
acquaintance Bekannte, Bekannter
acrimonious bitter
adjoining angrenzend
to adore über alles lieben
affection Zuneigung
agonised gequält
a great deal of eine Menge
a kindly thing etwas Nettes
to alight aussteigen
a litter of ein Haufen
a little way off etwas entfernt
all the trappings das ganze Drum und Dran
all very well: to be (was/were – been) all very well schön und gut sein
a long cascade of hair langes, wallendes Haar
a mouth like a button Knopfmund
angle Kante
anticipation Vorfreude
anxiety Sorge
any sort of so ein(e)
aplenty haufenweise
to approach zugehen auf
apron Schürze
to be (was/were – been) apt to be in der Regel … sein
arched: to be arched sich wölben
arm Ärmel
armour Rüstung
articled: to be (was/were – been) articled to in die Lehre gehen bei
a scattering of vereinzelt
as if on cue wie aufs Stichwort
as though there was all the time in the world als ob sie etc. alle Zeit der Welt hätten
as though to make up for something als eine Art Wiedergutmachung für etwas
to ask riddles Rätsel aufgeben
to ask someone out for dinner jemanden zum Abendessen einladen
to associate someone with something etwas mit jemandem in Verbindung bringen
at a day's notice von einem Tag auf den anderen
at an alarming rate beunruhigend schnell
at some peril to her own safety was nicht ungefährlich war
at the end of it am Ende
at the very mention of something bei der bloßen Erwähnung von etwas
attic Dachboden; im Dachgeschoss
attics Dachgeschoss
avenues of beech Buchenalleen
awestruck von Bewunderung ergriffen

awfully besonders; furchtbar
aye ja

## B

to baa blöken
to back away from someone von jemandem einen Schritt zurücktreten
back regions (of a house) Tiefen des Hauses
back to front: to be (was/were – been) back to front durcheinander sein
bairn Kind
baize Filz
baleful böse
ball of string Rolle Bindfaden
to bang a spoon on something mit einem Löffel gegen etwas schlagen
to bang on the door gegen die Tür schlagen
banister Geländer
bank Böschung
barbed mit Widerhaken versehen
bare: to be (was/were – been) bare nackt sein
bare-headed: to be (was/were – been) bare-headed barhäuptig sein
barrel Fass
basement Keller
battered verbeult
battlements Zinnen
bead curtain Perlenvorhang
beading Perlen
to beam down at someone jemanden anstrahlen
to bear (bore – borne) something etwas aushalten
beating: to be (was/were – been) beating vor sich hin schlagen
beauty spot schöner Fleck
to become (became – become) diminished klein werden
to become dynamic aktiv werden
bedspread Bettdecke
to beggar belief jeder Beschreibung spotten
belongings Sachen
beret Baskenmütze
besides außerdem
bill Schnabel
birds of a feather: to be (was/were – been) birds of a feather vom gleichen Schlag sein
biscuit tin Keksdose
bits of vereinzelt
blackberry day Brombeertag
blame: to be (was/were – been) to blame schuld sein
blast Tuten
blaze Glut
blazing lodernd
bleak trostlos
bleat Blöken
to blend with something sich in etwas einfügen
to be (was/were – been) blessed with something mit etwas gesegnet sein
blessedly wunderbar
blind Rollo
blink Blitz
bloody verdammt
blotting paper Löschpapier
bluntly geradeheraus
to blur together verschwimmen
boarding school Internat
bog Sumpf

to bolster something etwas Auftrieb geben
to bomb towards someone jemandem entgegenrasen
boost: to take (took – taken) a welcome boost wohltuend gestärkt werden
boot Kofferraum
border Grenze (zwischen England und Schottland)
border hedge of hawthorn begrenzende Weißdornhecke
bore Langweiler(in)
bored stiff: to be (was/were – been) bored stiff sich zu Tode langweilen
born and bred: to be (was/were – been) born and bred an einem Ort geboren und aufgewachsen sein, ein waschechter … sein, eine waschechte … sein
bothered: not be bothered to do something keine Lust haben, etwas zu tun
bottom Hosenboden
boudoir Ankleidezimmer
bouncy sprunghaft
bound for: to be (was/were – been) bound for auf dem Weg sein nach
bow Bug
bow tie Fliege
bowl Schale
bracken Adlerfarn
bramble thicket Brombeerdickicht
branch of spruce Fichtenzweig
brass bedstead Messingbettgestell
brass farthings: not appear to have two brass farthings to rub together keinen müden Pfennig zu besitzen scheinen
brass handle Messinggriff
to break (broke – broken) up zerbrechen
breaker Wellenbrecher
bright fröhlich
to bring (brought – brought) up the rear die Nachhut bilden
broken kaputt
broken-nailed die Fingernägel abgebrochen
bronze bronzefarben
brooch Brosche
bruised verletzt
to buck from the very idea sich schon bei dem Gedanken an etwas sträuben
buddy Kumpel
building Bauarbeiten
to bump down a lane einen Weg entlangrumpeln
bun Knoten
to bundle something out of one's mind etwas aus seinen Gedanken vertreiben
bunk Bett
burn Bach
to burst (burst – burst) into the forecourt auf den Hof brausen
to bustle with: the main street bustled with … auf der Hauptstraße herrschte ein reges Treiben mit …
button thread Knopflochgarn
by all accounts laut Berichten
by means of indem
by some stubborn contrivance durch sture Findigkeit
by the pavement am Bordstein

## C

to cable someone jemandem telegrafieren
calculating prüfend
to call it pax to Frieden schließen
called off: to be (was/were – been) called off abgesagt werden
canvas sneakers Leinenturnschuhe
capacious geräumig
caption Bildunterschrift
to care to think about something etwas wahrhaben wollen
to caress someone jemanden liebkosen
carrier bag Tragetüte
carved wood Holzschnitzerei
to cast (cast – cast) shadows Schatten werfen
casting Auswerfen der Angel
castlefuls of eine Burg voll(er)
casual ungezwungen
to catch (caught – caught) someone at something jemanden bei etwas erwischen
caterers Leute vom Partyservice
cattle grid Weidenrost
to be (was/were – been) caught unawares überrumpelt werden
cautiously vorsichtig
to cease one's grazing aufhören zu grasen
cedar tree Zeder
Certificate Zeugnis
chalet girl Zimmermädchen
chap Bursche
charming reizvoll
chartered accountant Wirtschaftsprüfer(in)
Cheers! Prost!
chest of drawers Kommode
to chew over something sich mit etwas auseinandersetzen
childhood fancy Kindheitstraum
chill Kälte
chilled: to be (was/were – been) chilled by the wind durch den Wind frösteln
chilling: to be (was/were – been) a chilling business keine schöne Angelegenheit sein
china Porzellan
choppy bewegt
chuckle Plätschern
chunk großes Stück
churlish: to be (was/were – been) churlish ungehörig sein
to churn something up etwas aufwühlen
circular stairs Wendeltreppe
to clamber down herunterklettern
clank Geklirr
to clear a room of furniture die Möbel aus einem Zimmer räumen
to clear up aufräumen
cleft: to be (was/were – been) cleft by durchschnitten werden von
close dicht
to be (was/were – been) close to someone jemandem nahe stehen
close-cropped kurz geschnitten
closet Schrank
clove Nelke
to cluster in Trauben hängen
coat hook Kleiderhaken
coated: to be (was/were – been) coated with mud verdreckt sein
cobbled ramp Auffahrt mit Kopfsteinpflaster

coiffure Frisur
to collect someone jemanden abholen
coloured bunt
column of newsprint Zeitungsspalte
to come (came – come) down to someone zu jemandem kommen
to come (came – come) loose sich lösen
to come out with something mit etwas herausrücken
to come towards someone zu jemandem kommen
to come upon someone auf jemanden treffen
commission Auftrag
to conform sich anpassen
conservatory Wintergarten
to construct something etwas zusammenstellen
contrivance Konstruktion
to contrive something etwas basteln
cooker Herd
corrie Kar
to cost (cost – cost) the earth ein Vermögen kosten
cottage pie Hackfleischauflauf
council Gemeinde
counter Ladentheke
country bumpkin Landpomeranze
country bus Überlandbus
courtship Romanze
courtyard Burghof
cowardice Feigheit
to crackle up knistern
craft Boot
cramped beengt
crate Kiste
to crave something sich nach etwas sehnen
crevice Spalte
crisp glatt
cross: to be (was/were – been) cross sauer sein
to cross the floor durchs Zimmer gehen
crow's feet Krähenfüße
to crumble to bits verfallen
to crumple sich verziehen
to cry (cried – cried) off einen Rückzieher machen
culinary kulinarisch
cultivator Kultivator
curlew Brachvogel
cut Schnitt
to cut (cut – cut) loose loslassen
to cut oneself off from someone sich von jemandem loslösen

## D

to dabble rumprobieren
daffodil Osterglocke
damask cloth Damasttischdecke
to dangle something etwas baumeln lassen
to dare someone mit jemandem wetten
darkly panelled dunkel getäfelt
darned gestopft
dashing todschick
daunting: to be (was/were – been) daunting beängstigend sein
deadly heftig
dear geliebt
death-watch beetle Klopfkäfer
deb Debütantin
dedicated mit Leib und Seele
deer fence Wildgatter

definite eindeutig
to defy someone sich jemandem widersetzen
delectable reizend
deliberately absichtlich
delighted: to be (was/were – been) delighted to hocherfreut sein, dass
demand Anforderung
derelict verfallen
to descend absteigen
to descend upon someone bei jemandem einfallen
despite oneself gegen seinen Willen
despite the fact that obwohl
to devise something etwas entwerfen
dicey riskant
to die sich legen
to die away leiser werden
to dig (dug – dug) something etwas umgraben
dignified würdevoll
dim trüb
dimple Grübchen
din-dins Fresschen
dinner jacket Smokingjacke
disastrous katastrophal
to disclose the fact that ergeben, dass
disconcerting irritierend
to disentangle oneself from something sich von etwas befreien
to disgorge something etwas entladen
dishes Geschirr
disinfectant Desinfektionsmittel
dismal trostlos
to disperse on something sich mit etwas zerstreuen
to dispose of something sich etwas entledigen
disreputable schäbig
to dissolve into something (e.g. laughter) in etwas ausbrechen (z. B. Gelächter)
distress Verzweiflung
distressed bekümmert
to do (did – done) a quick change of direction schnell abgeändert werden
to do for someone jemandem genügen
to do private nursing als Privatpflegerin arbeiten
to do something up etwas renovieren
dog biscuit Hundekuchen
dog meal Hundefutter
domestic häuslich
door of stripped pine abgebeizte Kiefernholztür
dot Punkt
to double something etwas verdoppeln
down-to-earth bodenständig
downy daunenweich
to drag one's gaze away from someone sich zwingen, von jemandem wegzuschauen
to dragoon someone into something jemanden mit Gewalt dazu bringen, etwas zu tun
draped: to be (was/were – been) draped verhüllt sein
draught Durchzug
to draw (drew – drawn) ziehen
to draw into einfahren nach
to draw someone physically away from someone jemanden regelrecht von jemandem wegziehen

to draw up anhalten
to draw up one's knees die Knie anziehen
dreaded plunge Sprung ins kalte Wasser
dressing table Frisierkommode
driech trostlos
drifts (of daffodils etc) Teppiche (von Osterglocken etc.)
driving peitschend
drooling sabbernd
to drop one's eyes den Blick senken
dry rot Trockenfäule
drystone-dyked von Trockensteinmauern umrahmt
to be (was/were – been) due back zurückkommen sollen
due: to be (was/were – been) due for a few days off ein paar Tage Urlaub haben
duly wie erwartet
dump Müllhalde
dusk was falling es dämmerte
dusky dämmerig
to dust something from something sich etwas von etwas wischen
dutifully gehorsam
dyke Mauer

## E

to ease a car gently up a ramp etc ein Auto ganz langsam eine Auffahrt etc. hochfahren
to ease something etwas lindern
easy unbefangen
ebb-tide beach Strand bei Ebbe
egg white Eiweiß
elaborate kunstvoll
elusive ausweichend; unerreichbar
embossed als Abdruck
embraced: to be (was/were – been) passionately embraced by someone von jemandem leidenschaftlich umarmt werden
embroidered bestickt
endings Abschiede
energetic aktiv
en fête: to be (was/were – been) en fête feiern
engaged: to be (was/were – been) engaged in conversation with someone mitten in einem Gespräch mit jemandem sein
engaging hinreißend
engrained with dirt mit tief sitzendem Schmutz
engrossed: to be (was/were – been) engrossed vertieft sein
to enlarge upon something näher auf etwas eingehen
enterprising unternehmungslustig
entourage Gefolge
er äh
'er (= her) ihr
erect aufrecht
establishment Wohnung
estate car Kombi
event for charity Wohltätigkeitsveranstaltung
evidence Zeichen
evocative Erinnerungen wachrufend
to exasperate someone jemanden auf die Palme bringen
exhausting anstrengend
experience Erlebnis

## F

fabric Material
to face someone jemanden ansehen

faded verblichen
faint leise
to fall (fell – fallen) silent schweigen
to fall (fell – fallen) to pieces baufällig sein; zugrunde gehen
familiar vertraut
family mementoes Familienandenken
fare Fahrgeld
to farm something etwas bewirtschaften
farmstead Gehöft
far-reaching: to be (was/were – been) far-reaching viele Reisen mit sich bringen
feared befürchtet
feature Note
to feed (fed – fed) someone jemanden bewirten
to feel (felt – felt) cross wütend sein
to feel for something nach etwas suchen
to feel numb with something taub vor etwas sein
to feel sick with jealousy krank vor Eifersucht sein
festive festlich
to fill something in etwas überbrücken
filthy dreckig
to find (found – found) oneself on the receiving end of someone's gaze feststellen, dass man von jemandem betrachtet wird
first-year student: to be (was/were – been) a first-year student im ersten Semester studieren
firth Förde
fishing-tackle shop Laden für Angelbedarf
fitted cupboard Einbauschrank
fixture Halterung
to flag müde werden
flagged: to be (was/were – been) flagged with something mit etwas gefliest sein
to flash funkeln
flattery Schmeicheleien
flock of sheep Schafherde
floorboard Diele
Florence Florenz
to flounder stammeln
flowered geblümt
flower-filled voller Blumen
flower stalk Blumenstiel
flummoxed: to be (was/were – been) flummoxed by something von etwas erschlagen sein
flurry: a flurry of Hektik
fly Fliege
to fly (flew – flown) overhead über jemanden hinwegfliegen
fold Falte
to fold up vorbei sein
foot Fuß (1 Fuß = 30,5 cm)
for a dare als Mutprobe
for all that trotzdem
forebear Vorfahre
forecourt Hof
for the last time ever zum allerletzten Mal
fragrant duftend
framed: to be (was/were – been) framed eingerahmt sein
frankness Offenheit
frantic: to be (was/were – been) frantic außer sich sein
freckled sommersprossig
free rein: to be (was/were – been) able to allow one's thoughts a

free rein seinen Gedanken freien Lauf lassen können
French window Terrassentür
frightfully beeindruckend
frilled curtain Rüschenvorhang
from beyond something hinter etwas hervor
from the first von Anfang an
frying brutzelnd
fuel Brennstoff
furry weich

## G

Gaelic gälisch
gallery Galerie
gang Gruppe
gangling schlaksig
to gape jemanden mit offenem Mund anstarren
garden netting Gartennetz
gatehouse Pförtnerhaus
gateway Tor
gathering zunehmend
General Stores Gemischtwarenladen
genuinely wirklich
to get (got – got) a divorce sich scheiden lassen
to get around to doing something dazu kommen, etwas zu tun
to get chucked out rausgeworfen werden
to get drunk sich betrinken
to get one's hackles up seine Stacheln aufstellen
to get someone over someone jemandem über jemanden hinweghelfen
to get the bit between one's teeth sich etwas in den Kopf setzen
ghastly furchtbar
giant-sized riesig
gingerbread Pfefferkuchen mit Ingwergeschmack
to give (gave – given) a derisory laugh spöttisch lachen
to give someone a hand with something jemandem bei etwas helfen
to give someone a ring jemanden anrufen
to give someone one of one's most persuasive smiles jemandem eines seiner verführerischsten Lächeln schenken
to give someone's hand a pat jemandem einen Klaps auf die Hand geben
to give someone the sack jemanden entlassen
gladly gerne
glamour Glanz
glass-fronted cabinet Glasvitrine
to gleam with something vor etwas funkeln
to glean something from something etwas etwas entnehmen
gloom Bedrückung
to go (went – gone) fahren
to go ahead vorfahren
to go blackberrying Brombeeren pflücken gehen
to go on about something weiter von etwas erzählen
to go ting „Ting" machen
to go to a lot of effort to do something sich große Mühe geben, etwas zu tun
to go with something eine Begleiterscheinung von etwas sein
godchild Patenkind

God-given day Bilderbuchtag
... that's going ..., das es gibt
good: to not be (was/were – been) any good keinen Zweck haben
gooseberry Stachelbeere
grand prachtvoll
grant Darlehen
to grapple with something mit etwas kämpfen
grassy grasbewachsen
grate Kamin
gratitude Dankbarkeit
grave ernst
gravel terrace kiesbestreute Terrasse
gravy Soße
to graze weiden
greengrocer Gemüsehändler(in)
to grind (ground – ground) one's way up mühsam hochächzen
grinding knirschend
to grit one's teeth die Zähne zusammenbeißen
grubby mark Schmutzfleck
to guddle for something mit den Händen etwas fangen
guess: to not be (was/were – been) able to guess something etwas nicht erahnen können
gunwale Dollbord
gust Schwall

## H

half-landing Treppenabsatz
to halt anhalten
handkerchief Taschentuch
to handle something very neatly etwas super hinkriegen
handsome schön
to hang (hung – hung) on to something an etwas festhalten
to hang out of a window aus einem Fenster lehnen
hard-wearing strapazierfähig
to have (had – had) a life to make for oneself seinen eigenen Weg finden müssen
to have friends in Freunde zu Besuch haben
to have got a point recht haben
to have got years to go yet noch viele Jahre vor sich haben
to have no place nicht vorgesehen sein
to have one's eye on something auf etwas ein Auge geworfen haben
to have some attention paid to oneself beachtet werden
to have the sense to do something so klug sein, etwas zu tun
to have the wit to do something so schlau sein, etwas zu tun
haversacked: to be (was/were – been) haversacked mit Rucksäcken ausgerüstet sein
to head to nach ... fahren
head: to be (was/were – been) way over someone's head jemanden völlig überfordern
headlight Scheinwerfer
headline Schlagzeile
headscarf Kopftuch
heather-clad heidekrautbewachsen
heathery heidekrautbewachsen
to heave oneself off something sich von etwas hieven
Heavens! Du liebe Zeit!
heavily stark; üppig
heavy schwer

heel Endstück
heel of one's hand Handballen
hefty deftig; kräftig
helplessly hilflos
Her hair was silky black. Sie hatte seidiges, schwarzes Haar.
hessian aus Sackleinen
hideous scheußlich
high-pitched schrill
high-powered erfolgreich
high-rise flat Hochhaus
high-walled von hohen Mauern umgeben
hillside Hang
his temper was rising to match her own seine Wut wurde genauso groß wie ihre
to hitch a lift trampen
to hold (held – held) someone at arm's length jemanden von sich weghalten
to hook a fish einen Fisch am Haken haben
hoose Haus
horn Hupe
hospital drama Krankenhausserie
hothouse London flower Londoner Gewächshauspflanze
hovering: with laughter hovering immer zum Lachen bereit
to howl brüllen
howling heulend
hugely patterned groß gemustert
humdrum alltäglich
humiliation Demütigung
to hurry away es eilig haben
hurt Schmerz
hybrid rhododendrons Rhododendronkreuzungen

## I

I can't handle it. Das packe ich nicht.
icy eiskalt
to idle verweilen
idleness Muße
imaginary imaginär
inadequate unzureichend
in anticipation gespannt
in a whisper of satin skirts mit raschelnden Satinröcken
in bud: to be (was/were – been) in bud Knospen treiben
incestuous inzestuös
incline Steigung
incongruous fehl am Platz
inconsequent belanglos
inconsistence Ungereimtheit
incredulous ungläubig
in deference to something aus Respekt vor etwas
indicative: to be (was/were – been) indicative ein deutlicher Hinweis sein
indomitable unbezwingbar
inevitable: the inevitable das Unvermeidliche
inevitably zwangsläufig
infirm gebrechlich
to inflict something etwas zufügen
in hand zu erledigend
in heat and haste in der Hitze des Gefechts
inland landeinwärts
insane verrückt
in sight in Sichtweite
instant Augenblick
in stockinged feet in Strümpfen

in that sludgy green colour in diesem Schlammgrün
in total puzzlement völlig verblüfft
to introduce somebody jemanden vorstellen
irrepressible unverwüstlich
irresponsible verantwortungslos
It's agony. Es tut weh.

## J

jangling Klingeln
jelly Gelee
jewelled juwelenbesetzt
job lot Restposten
job of work Arbeit
to join something in etwas eintreten
junk yard Schrottplatz
just nur
just a few little touches nur noch der letzte Schliff
just as well ist auch nötig
juvenile kindisch

## K

keel Kiel
keenly eindringlich
kilt Kilt
Kirk Kirche
kitchen landing Absatz vor der Küche
kneeler Kniekissen
to know (knew – known) a nudge of doubt leise Zweifel verspüren
to know a stirring of feminine irritation sich bewusst werden, dass sich die Frau in einem ärgert
to know how to do something etwas können

## L

lace front Spitzenvorderteil
Lachlan grapevine Gerüchteküche von Lachlan
ladybird Marienkäfer
landing Treppenabsatz
lap Absatz
lapel Aufschlag
to lapse auslaufen
larch Lärche
large-footed mit großen Füßen
to last durchhalten
latch Riegel
to lead (led – led) someone with a carrot jemanden mit Zuckerbrot locken
leak undichte Stelle
to leap (lept – lept) at someone jemandem entgegenspringen
to learn (learnt – learnt) a trade einen Beruf erlernen
leathery zäh
to leave (left – left) someone in the lurch jemanden hängen lassen
left: to be (was/were – been) left to one's own devices sich selbst überlassen werden
to let (let – let) go of something etwas loslassen
let-down Enttäuschung
to lie (lay – lain) daliegen
to lie like a log wie ein Stück Holz daliegen
light-hearted unbekümmert
like a great ribbon wie ein breites Band
like a lunatic als ob ich etc. nicht ganz bei Sinnen war
to limp along dahinplätschern
line Falte

lined: to be (was/were – been) lined with something mit etwas gefüttert sein
linen aus Leinen
litter of Abfälle von
to live out something etwas verbringen
living creature lebendiges Wesen
loch See
lofty hoch
log Scheit
log fire Holzfeuer
that was why I've been so long in … deswegen hat es so lange gedauert, bis ich …
long-suffering schwer geprüft
to look about oneself sich umsehen
to look amazingly like someone jemandem unglaublich ähnlich sehen
to look plain unattraktiv aussehen
to look sulky aussehen, als ob man beleidigt ist
to loom sich erheben
loose cover Schonbezug
love Schatz
loved: to be (was/were – been) loved on the rebound from some other person von jemandem geliebt werden, der noch nicht über jemand anderen hinweg ist
to lower oneself down sich setzen
low-necked tief ausgeschnitten
low-waisted mit tief angesetzter Taille
lulled: to be (was/were – been) lulled by something von etwas eingelullt werden
luncheon Mittagessen
to lurk lauern

## M

maddened: to be (was/were – been) maddened sich totärgern
maddening zum Verrücktwerden
to make a snap judgment vorschnell urteilen
to make (made – made) for the door zur Tür gehen
to make no apologies sich nicht entschuldigen
to make oneself evident zum Vorschein kommen
to make someone feel embarrassed jemandem peinlich sein
to make the great commitment sich ernsthaft binden
make-believe imaginär
make-shift behelfsmäßig
malleable anschmiegsam
manhandled: to be (was/were – been) manhandled verfrachtet werden
Manse Pfarrhaus
mantelpiece Kaminsims
marvel Wunder
marvellous unheimlich nett; wunderbar
massive riesig
mate Kumpel
to materialise sich finden
mature reif
maze Gewirr
to mean (meant – meant) to be something etwas sein wollen
to mean well es gut meinen
meant: to be (was/were – been) meant to do something etwas tun sollen
meantime inzwischen

medieval mittelalterlich
to meet (met – met) a challenge sich einer Herausforderung stellen
to meet someone's gaze jemandes Blick begegnen
to meet someone jemanden abholen
memorable denkwürdig
mended ausgebessert
met: I was met by … mir schlug … entgegen
millions of teeming insects Gewimmel von Millionen von Insekten
mind zwar
mind: she never minded es machte ihr nie etwas aus
minister Pfarrer, Pfarrerin
mint sauce Minzsoße
mist Nebel
misty: to be (was/were – been) misty with condensation beschlagen sein
model mother vorbildliche Mutter
money-broker Finanzmakler(in)
money-making einträglich
mooring Anlegeplatz
to mop someone up jemandem die Tränen vom Gesicht wischen
moral courage Zivilcourage
moss Moos
motorway Autobahn
mounted aufgezogen
to mourn for something etwas nachtrauern
to move on weiterziehen
much mehrfach
mud Matsch
muggy schwül
to munch genteelly on something vornehm auf etwas kauen
mural Wandgemälde
murk dicker Nebel
musky moschusartig
musty moderig
mutual gemeinsam
My! Du meine Güte!

## N

to nail one's flags to the mast seine Flaggen hissen
narrow schmal
national überregional
neck Hals
neckline Ausschnitt
to net something out of the water etwas aus dem Wasser fischen
to never fail to make someone laugh jemanden immer wieder zum Lachen bringen
newsagent Zeitungshändler(in)
newsprint Druckerschwärze
nicely gut
nip Hauch
no good: to be no good keinen Zweck haben
No man is an island. Niemand ist eine Insel.
no' nicht; kein
not anticipating nichts ahnend
not in the least kein bisschen
novelty Neues
nuisance: to be (was/were – been) a nuisance allen auf die Nerven gehen
nursery Kinderzimmer
nursing: to be (was/were – been) nursing als Pfleger/Pflegerin arbeiten

## O

to oblige with something mit etwas dienen
occasion Anlass
odd skurril
of sorts eine Art
off: to be (was/were – been) off geplatzt sein
off: we're off es geht los
on the edge: to be (was/were – been) on the edge of tears kurz davor sein zu weinen
on the far side of auf der anderen Seite von
only aber
to operate arbeiten
opulence Pracht
ordinary durchschnittlich
ounce Fünkchen
out of von … aus
out of: to be (was/were – been) out of something kein(e) mehr haben
out of date: to be (was/were – been) very out of date gar nicht auf dem Laufenden sein
out of humour: to be (was/were – been) out of humour schlechte Laune haben
out of mind aus dem Sinn
out of the dazzle aus dem grellen Licht
out on the battlements im Freien auf den Zinnen
outbuildings Nebengebäude
outdone: to not be (was/were – been) outdone nicht zurückstehen wollen
overcast bedeckt
to overtake (overtook – overtaken) someone jemanden überholen
oyster-catcher Austernfänger

## P

pack Horde
pagan heidnisch
painstakingly sorgfältig
painter Fangleine
pair of steps Trittleiter
panelled getäfelt
panting hechelnd
paper-chase Schnitzeljagd
paraffin Paraffin
paranoically paranoisch
party of friends Gruppe von Freunden
passageway Gang
pastry scraps Teigfetzen
patch Stelle
patched geflickt
pathetically erbärmlich
a patter of drops Regentropfen
to pause innehalten
pearl stud Perlenohrstecker
peaty torfig
peaty tang Torfgeruch
pebble Kiesel
pebble jewellery Bergkristallschmuck
to peer at something short-sightedly etwas mit kurzsichtigen Augen angestrengt anschauen
to people bevölkern
perceptive wahrnehmungsfähig
persistent beharrlich
petite zierlich
to picture something sich etwas vorstellen
piercingly cold bitterkalt
piggery Schweinestall

pig-headed dickköpfig
pile of bricks Ziegelsteinhaufen
pillared window Säulenfenster
pillowcase Kissenbezug
pinafore Kittelschürze
pine Kiefer
pine dresser Anrichte aus Kiefernholz
plane Ebene
plank Brett
planking of the boat Bootsplanken
to plant a peck on someone's cheek jemandem ein Küsschen auf die Wange geben
plaster moulding Gipsornament
plaster trough Gipstrog
pliers Kneifzange
ploy Vergnügen; Betätigung
plucky: to be (was/were – been) plucky mutig sein
to plumb senkrecht stehen
plum-bloom lila blühend
pointless: to be (was/were – been) pointless sinnlos sein
polish Möbelpolitur
polished glänzend
polished: to be (was/were – been) polished to a sheen auf Hochglanz poliert sein
pond Teich
ponderous schwerfällig
pool of mud Schlammpfütze
poppet Schätzchen
porch Veranda
pork-butcher Schweinemetzger(in)
porter Gepäckträger
pot plant Topfpflanze
pounding Hämmern
pouter-pigeon bosom Kropftaubenbusen
pressing dringend
pretty enough ziemlich hübsch
prevailing vorherrschend
priceless von unschätzbarem Wert
pristine klar
private eigen
to proceed to do something sich daranmachen, etwas zu tun
to prompt someone to do something jemanden dazu veranlassen, etwas zu tun
proper richtig
properly richtig
prospect of Aussicht auf
to protrude from something aus etwas hervorragen
to provide for something für etwas sorgen
provided vorausgesetzt
provocative kess
prudent umsichtig
to pull it all together das Ruder herumreißen
to pull something down etwas abreißen
to pull something up etwas hochziehen
to put (put – put) in an appearance sich sehen lassen
to put on speed beschleunigen
to put something out of one's mind etwas aus seinen Gedanken verbannen
to put something straight etwas in Ordnung bringen
puzzled verwirrt

## Q

to quarrel with someone mit jemandem zanken

quarry tile Sandsteinfliese
quilted waistcoat Steppweste
quilting Quilten

## R

rage Zorn
ragged mitgenommen
railway track Eisenbahnschiene
ranged: to be (was/were – been) ranged verteilt sein
rank absolut
rather ziemlich
rat-race Konkurrenzkampf
to rattle rattern
ray Strahl
razorbill Tordalk
to reach up sich recken
recalcitrant widerspenstig; aufsässig
to recall the pleasure of something daran denken, wie man sich gefreut hatte
receiver Hörer
recess Nische
recognition dawned in someone's face man sah, dass sie etc. mich etc. erkannte
Recognition sparked. Sie etc. erkannte sie etc.
redoubtable Respekt einflößend
reedy schilfig
reel Reel
to reel something in etwas einholen
relations Verwandte
to remain constant to someone jemandem treu bleiben
remains Überreste
remand home Jugendstrafanstalt
remembered unvergessen
reminded: to be (was/were – been) reminded of something an etwas erinnert werden
to respond to the spur auf die Peitsche reagieren
revealed: to be (was/were – been) revealed zum Vorschein kommen
to ring (rang – rung) someone jemanden anrufen
to ring someone up jemanden anrufen
to ring with voices and laughter von Stimmen und Gelächter hallen
ripe: to be (was/were – been) ripe with something voll von etwas sein
to rivet something to something etwas an etwas anbringen
roasted gebraten
robe Morgenmantel
roll Brötchen
roof tiles Dachziegel
rosy rosarot
to round something um etwas herumfahren
row Streit
to rub someone up the wrong way bei jemandem anecken
to rub something clear sich etwas frei wischen
to rub something off etwas abschmirgeln
rubber boots Gummistiefel
rubber-heeled gummibesohlt
ruefully voll Bedauern
to ruffle someone's hair jemandes Haar zerzausen
rugger pitch Rugbyfeld
to rummage in something in etwas kramen

to run (ran – run) a mental finger down something etwas im Kopf durchgehen
to run something etwas betreiben; etwas leiten
to run wild herumtoben
Rural Landfrauenverein
rush mat Binsenmatte
to rustle rascheln
to rustle up something etwas auftreiben
rutted ausgefahren

## S

sagging halb aus den Angeln hängend
saint Engel
salt mines: to be (was/were – been) worse than the salt mines schlimmer als Zwangsarbeit sein
sated: to be (was/were – been) sated with something sich an etwas satt gegessen haben
satiny seidig
Saturday finery Ausgehkleidung
save for außer
to savour something etwas auskosten
to saw (sawed – sawn) sägen
to say (said – said) unforgivably etwas Unverzeihliches sagen
scarcely kaum
scarlet scharlachrot
scent Duft
to scent something etwas wittern
scheme Plan
school outing Schulausflug
schoolmaster's family Lehrerfamilie
to scramble over something über etwas klettern
scrap Stückchen
scrap merchant Schrotthändler(in)
scraped: to be (was/were – been) scraped back into a ponytail zu einem Pferdeschwanz zurückgebunden sein
scratched: to be (was/were – been) scratched zerkratzt sein
screaming sensationsheischend
scream of fury Wutschrei
scree Geröll
screwed: to be (was/were – been) screwed into something zu etwas gedreht sein
seated ausgebeult
sea urchin Seeigel
seaweed Seetang
secateurs Gartenschere
second time around zweiter Anlauf
to see (saw – seen) it through durchhalten
to see someone jemanden besuchen
to see someone through something jemandem über etwas hinweghelfen
to see something etwas verstehen
to seek (sought – sought) someone out jemanden ausfindig machen
self-esteem Selbstwertgefühl
self-respecting der/die etwas auf sich hält
to send (sent – sent) someone packing jemanden hinauswerfen
sensible vernünftig
to separate sich teilen
serene heiter
to set eyes on somebody jemanden zu Gesicht bekommen
set free: to be (was/were – been) set free die Freiheit geschenkt bekommen

set-to Krach
shambles: to be (was/were – been) in a state of shambles in einem schlimmen Zustand sein
to share a flat mit jemandem eine Wohnung teilen
sharpness Schärfe
Sharp on time. Auf die Minute.
shattered: to be (was/were – been) shattered by something durch etwas erschüttert werden
shindig Remmidemmi
to ship the oars die Riemen einziehen
shooting jacket Jagdrock
shore Ufer
shortbread crumb Butterkekskrümel
shortcoming Fehler
shorthand Stenografie
to shoulder something etwas auf sich nehmen
to shove something around etwas herumschieben
showpiece Paradestück
to shrug mit den Achseln zucken
shuffling schlurfend
shunted: to be (was/were – been) shunted to and fro hin- und hergeschoben werden
shutter Fensterladen
sick: He'll make himself sick. Ihm wird schlecht werden.
sickle of shingle kleiner Kiesstrand
silhouetted als Silhouette
silver birch Weißbirke
skating party Schlittschuhparty
to skim across the water übers Wasser schießen
skinny mager
sky-light Oberlicht
to slam zuknallen
to slap plätschern
to slap a preservation order on something etwas unter Denkmalschutz stellen
sleeper Nachtzug
slender schlank
slightly ein bisschen
slip of nature Ausrutscher der Natur
slipper satin Atlasseide
slit window Gusserker
slope Hang; Schräge
smear of something verschmierter Fleck von etwas
to smile broadly übers ganze Gesicht lächeln
smoky rauchig
to smooth something down etwas glatt streichen
smouldering glimmernd
smug selbstzufrieden
snagged: to be (was/were – been) snagged Fäden gezogen haben
to snake away sich schlängeln
snapped up: to be (was/were – been) snapped up weggeschnappt werden
snapshot Schnappschuss
snifter Gläschen
so … as to so … dass
So what. Na und.
soaring hoch
Social Diary Gesellschaftsseite
social visiting Höflichkeitsbesuche
sodden nass
sole einzig
solicitor Rechtsanwalt, Rechtsanwältin
solitary einsam

sophisticated kultiviert
to sort out one's own mess for oneself sich am eigenen Schopf aus dem Sumpf ziehen
to sort something out sich um etwas kümmern
sough Rauschen
sound Geräusch
to sound sich anhören wie
sound: he made it sound ... bei ihm hörte es sich ... an
speaker Lautsprecher
spectre Gespenst
spell-binding fesselnd
to spin (spun – spun) someone jemanden drehen
to spin something out etwas in die Länge ziehen
splendour Pracht
Spode hochwertiges englisches Porzellan
to sport anhaben
spray Zweig
to spring-clean Frühjahrsputz machen
spiral staircase Wendeltreppe
to sprout with wuchern
to square something with someone etwas mit jemandem absprechen
square-chinned mit eckigem Kinn
squat gedrungen
stained gefärbt
stained: to be (was/were – been) stained verfärbt sein
stale verbraucht
stalwart tüchtig
stand Gruppe
to stand (stood – stood) someone dinner jemanden zum Abendessen einladen
to start anspringen
to start running down: the mill started running down mit der Spinnerei ging es bergab
to start up the engine den Motor anlassen
startled: to be (was/were – been) startled erschrocken sein
startled: to be (was/were – been) startled into immobility zur Salzsäule erstarren
startling verblüffend
state of mind Verfassung
staunchly unerschütterlich
to stay out of touch nichts von sich hören lassen
steady gleichmäßig
steepening steiler werdend
to stick (stuck – stuck) something out etwas durchhalten
to stick to something an etwas festhalten
sticky klebrig
stolid phlegmatisch
stone aus Stein
to stoop sich bücken
stooped gebeugt
stopping in jedem Dorf anhaltend
to stow something etwas verstauen
straggling unordentlich; auseinandergezogen
to straighten up sich aufrichten
strand Strang
strands of grey graue Strähnen
strath Tal
to strike (struck – struck) einschlagen; entgegenschlagen
the hallway struck with a damp chill im Flur schlug ihm eine feuchte Kälte entgegen

a string of something ein Haufen von etwas
to strip something off etwas abbeizen
stroke Schlaganfall, Schlag
strong-featured markant
to be (was/were – been) studded in something in etwas gekleidet sein
to study French seine Französischkenntnisse erweitern
to study something sich etwas genau ansehen
subject Thema
Such comfort. So tröstlich.
to suit someone jemandem stehen
summit Gipfel
supper Abendessen
suspended: to be (was/were – been) suspended from something von etwas herunterhängen
suspicious argwöhnisch
sweater Pullover
to sweep (swept – swept) down sanft abfallen
to sweep someone up in someone's wake jemanden mit sich mitreißen
to sweep something up etwas schwungvoll hochheben
swinging door Pendeltür

## T

tabloid Boulevardzeitung
tacked on: to be (was/were – been) tacked on angebaut sein
tail-waving schwanzwedelnd
to take (took – taken) a drink einen heben
to take notice of someone jemanden zur Kenntnis nehmen
to take off for sich nach … absetzen
to take off one's hat to someone den Hut vor jemandem ziehen
to take on too much sich zu viel aufladen
to take one's bearings sich orientieren
to take oneself off davongehen
to take something for granted etwas für selbstverständlich halten
to take something in etwas umfassen
to take the right course den richtigen Weg einschlagen
to take up farming Bauer werden, Bäuerin werden
to take up residence einziehen
Tales of the Vienna Woods Geschichten aus dem Wienerwald
tall hoch
tattered abgegriffen; ausgefranst
tawny goldbraun
tear-brimmed in Tränen schwimmend
to tease someone jemanden quälen
teeming glut of humanity wuselnde Schwemme der Menschheit
to tend something sich um etwas kümmern
tentatively zögernd
that last summer of all in jenem letzten Sommer
the best part of one's life fast sein ganzes Leben lang
the face of the hills die Berghänge
the lot of you euch/ihr alle
the one who led the way der Anführer, die Anführerin

the Services die Streitkräfte
the very next day gleich am nächsten Tag
the world our etc. oyster die Welt stand uns etc. offen
there came a tap at his door es klopfte an seiner Tür
there is nothing more letting down than es ist nichts enttäuschender als
there was an air of … about him er strahlte … aus
there was another bite or two es bissen noch einer oder zwei an
there was no way it could carry on es konnte unmöglich so weitergehen
these days heutzutage
to think (thought – thought) of something sich etwas vorstellen
to think something beautiful etc. etwas schön etc. finden
third-rate drittklassig
threadbare abgetreten
throb of life Puls des Lebens
to thump down on plumpsen auf
thundering dahindonnernd
thwart Ruderbank
to tidy something etwas in Ordnung bringen
to tidy something up etwas aufräumen
to tie something with a flourish of gold ribbon etwas mit einem aufwendigen Goldband zusammenbinden
Tight lines! Petri Heil!
to tilt one's face das Gesicht neigen
tip-tilted stupsig
tireless unermüdlich
tiresome lästig
to boot obendrein
toddler Kleinkind
to toe something off etwas abstreifen
tomboy jungenhaft
tongue-and-grooved mit Spundung
ton-up der/die/das 100 Meilen pro Stunde fährt
top step oberste Stufe
to toss something etwas werfen
to totter tapsen
to touch stone auf Grund laufen
touching: to be (was/were – been) touching bewegend sein
tough zäh
to trail hinter jemandem herziehen
trailing ivy Efeuranken
trainers Turnschuhe
trainy clothes Reiseklamotten
tranquilly gelassen
tray of Tablett mit
tremendously spotted stark getüpfelt
tremor Beben
trolley Gepäckwagen
troop off to abziehen
trouble: to be (was/were – been) more trouble than one is worth mehr Ärger machen, als man wert ist
trout Forelle
to trundle schieben
trunk Schrankkoffer
truth be told um ehrlich zu sein
to try (tried – tried) hard sein Bestes geben
to tuck something away in something etwas in etwas stecken

turf Gras
to turn werden
to turn on one's heel sich auf dem Absatz umdrehen
to turn someone into something aus jemandem etwas machen
to turn stale schal werden
to turn the corner of a street um die Ecke fahren und in eine Straße einbiegen
to turn to stone einfrieren
to turn up sich blicken lassen
turn: to be (was/were – been) someone's turn to do something an der Reihe sein, etwas zu tun
turned out: to be (was/were – been) turned out herausgeworfen werden
turning Abzweigung
turquoise türkisfarben
turreted with pepper-pot towers mit Zwiebeltürmchen
tussock Büschel
tweeter Hochtonlautsprecher
twice someone's age doppelt so alt wie jemand
twisted: to be (was/were – been) twisted verdreht sein
type Schrift

## U

unacknowledged uneingestanden
unattainable: to be (was/were – been) unattainable unerreichbar sein
unblinking unverwandt
unblinking: her eyes were unblinking Sie schaute ihn unverwandt an.
unchecked unbeaufsichtigt
uncompromising eigenwillig
to undo (undid – undone) the wrappings ein Geschenk auspacken
undying unsterblich
unfashionably unmodern
union Verbindung
unpredictability Unberechenbarkeit
unremarkable wenig bemerkenswert
unresolved ungelöst
to unroll sich ausbreiten
unsophisticated schlicht
untroubled unbekümmert
utterly ausgesprochen

## V

vagaries Wechselfälle
valerian Baldrian
varnish Lack
to varnish something etwas lackieren
vastly patient mit Engelsgeduld
very gerade
to view something at a distance etwas aus der Ferne betrachten
vital lebendig
voices mingling Stimmengewirr
to volunteer something etwas preisgeben
vulnerable verletzlich

## W

to walk away from someone jemanden verlassen
to walk dogs Hunde ausführen
wallflower Goldlack
to waltz Walzer tanzen

warming strides Schritte, die einen aufwärmen
to watch out for someone sich um jemanden kümmern
to wear (wore – worn) someone out jemandem zu anstrengend sein
weather-seamed wettergegerbt
weaves Gewebe
wee klein
to weight the line die Angel beschweren
weightless unbedeutend
welcoming einladend
well-bred distinguiert
wet through völlig durchnässt
what with womit
wheelbarrow Schubkarren
whirlwind stürmisch
to whistle pfeifen
to whistle for something etwas herbeipfeifen
window box Blumenkasten
wine-dark tintenschwarz
to winkle oneself away from a place sich von einem Ort loseisen
wire hanger Drahtbügel
wiry drahtig
wise weise
wistfully wehmütig
with a distant view of mit Blick auf … in der Ferne
with access zu erreichen
with energies to spare mit überschüssiger Energie
with little fuss ohne viel Aufhebens
with that daraufhin
within yards bis auf mehrere Yard
Women's Rural Institute Landfrauenverein
woofer Tieftonlautsprecher
wool broker Wollhändler(in)
woollen hat Wollmütze
woollen mill Wollspinnerei
wordless: to be (was/were – been) wordless sprachlos sein
to work out klappen
workforce Belegschaft
workrooms Werkstatt
worn abgetragen
worry Sorge
to worsen sich verschlechtern
wound up: to be (was/were – been) wound up aufgezogen sein
wreath Kranz
wretched gemein
wrist Handgelenk
to write (wrote – written) something down to something etwas als etwas abschreiben
wrought-iron schmiedeeisern
wryly ironisch

## Y

yard Yard (1 Yard = 0,91 Meter)

## Z

zipped mit Reißverschluss